WHERE ARCHITECTS STAY IN THE ALPS

LODGINGS
FOR
DESIGN
ENTHUSIASTS

SIBYLLE KRAMER

WHERE ARCHITECTS STAY IN THE ALPS

LODGINGS
FOR
DESIGN
ENTHUSIASTS

BRAUN

Contents

Contents

Anakolodge surrounded by the Swiss Alps. Alpine Shelter Skuta in the Slovenian mountains.

Preface

People always have been fascinated by mountains. They serve as source of energy and are symbol of freedom, the perfect place to take a deep break, for self-discovery, to embark on a great adventure or to take on a physical challenge. There are nature and wildlife, vision and inspiration, physical activity, tranquility, and relaxation far away from the hustle and bustle of the city. Based on the success of the volumes "Where Architects Stay", "Where Architects Stay in Europe", and "Where Architects Stay in Germany", this new volume, focused on the Alps, meets the readers' wishes for a geographically denser architectural travel guide.

The Alps are the largest mountain range in Central Europe, stretching some 200,000 square kilometers across France, Monaco, Italy, Switzerland, Germany, Liechtenstein, Austria, and Slovenia, and including 128 mountains above 4,000 meters – most notably Mont Blanc, which rises 4,809 meters into the sky. The current book features 48 wonderful lodgings of great and consistent architectural concepts, set in that fascinating alpine setting.

The architecture is in dialogue with the mountains, and sometimes looks archaically rough, wooden, and close to nature, or contrasts with delicate design. The design and layout of the houses each tell an individual story, reflect their connection with the mountains and their individual design characteristics. Hence, roof shapes

Freiform Private Guesthouse with a view of the mountains. Infinity pool at Miramonti Boutique Hotel. Exterior view of Odles Lodge.

are inspired by mountain peaks, colors by the surroundings, and façade openings by the captivating views. The buildings quote traditional construction forms and uses and interpret them in a modern way, thus establish a historical connection to the place on the one hand and a modern, warm, and comfortable atmosphere on the other. All buildings featured in this volume, characterized by a sustainable use of resources and respect for nature, are based on very different, but always unique, individual, and excellent concepts and high standards. These lodgings offer, together with the breathtaking landscapes, that ensures a wide range of active and relaxing leisure, the opportunity to enjoy an unforgettable stay.

INFORMATION. ARCHITECTS> NOA*
NETWORK OF ARCHITECTURE // 2017.
HOTEL> 6 MINI CHALETS WITH 4
ROOMS EACH // 23 SQM EACH ROOM
// 2 GUESTS EACH ROOM. ADDRESS>
ALPE DI SIUSI, SALTRIA, ITALY.
WWW.ZALLINGER.COM

Zallinger

SALTRIA, ITALY

The Zallinger is an example of best practice in the treatment of a historic structure in a landscape of great value. Traditional forms and materials are embraced and reinterpreted to satisfy the concept of hospitality with high standards of sustainability, design quality and comfort. The 19th-century barns were architecturally given a new life as mini chalets. They recreate the charm of an alpine village and provide new spaces without altering the existing volumes.

The architects, inspired by the structure of old barns, designed an exterior wall cladding of solid wood blocks for the chalets. The panels in front of the large windows open revealing a view of the spectacular alpine landscape. The façade cladding has a uniform look and provides a magical light effect. The interior is dominated by warm and natural materials, such as natural larch wood and loden fabrics in combination with resource-saving furnishings.

Beautiful details show time and again that Zallinger and its architects paid attention to nature, mountains and to sustainability. For instance, the connecting paths between the chalets and the hut are not illuminated to avoid light pollution and to give guests who are equipped with lanterns the opportunity to enjoy the magic of the starry sky.

Exterior façade. Detail of the relaxation area.
Interior view of the custom-made furniture.
Exterior view of the chalets surrounded by snow.

Room with a central glass shower. Detail of the sauna
with large window. Exterior view of the façade.
Floor plan, Interior view of one of the rooms.

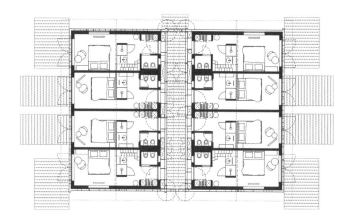

GETTING AROUND. THE ZALLINGER
IS LOCATED NEXT TO THE SKI SLOPE
OF THE ALPE DI SIUSI AND IS ALSO
FREQUENTED BY EXTERNAL GUESTS
FOR DINNER AND RELAXATION.
ON THE PANORAMIC TERRACE
YOU CAN ENJOY ALL DAY LONG
TYPICAL DELICACIES PREPARED
FROM REGIONAL AND SEASONAL
INGREDIENTS. FOR IN-HOUSE
GUESTS, THE ZALLINGER ALSO
OFFERS A SAUNA WITH A VIEW
OF THE MOUNTAINSCAPE.

INFORMATION. ARCHITECTS> PEDEVILLA ARCHITECTS + ARCH. CAROLINE WILLEIT // 2013. HOUSE> 200 SQM // 6–8 GUESTS // 2 BEDROOMS // 1 BATHROOM. ADDRESS> PLISCIA 13, ENNEBERG MAREBBE, SOUTH TYROL, ITALY. WWW.LAPEDEVILLA.IT

Chalet la Pedevilla

SOUTH TYROL, ITALY

The cultural landscape of the Val Badia in the heart of the Dolomites is characterized by a large number of hamlets called "viles". These constitute a small group of farms based on a close structure. Unlike the individual farms, their purpose is to form a community of neighbors who support each other and provide basic agricultural services to the families living in the "vila".

Chalet la Pedevilla is located at an altitude of 1,280 meters above sea level, in the hamlet of Enneberg, and has been designed including the building tradition of the "viles". The two offset structures carefully inserted into the slope correspond to the local type of farmhouses that consists of two buildings. Typical regional ornaments and other characteristic elements, such as the gable roof, loggia and wooden façade, are integrated and reinterpreted in a clear and individual way. In order to create a protective, homely and familiar interior, cozy Swiss stone pinewood and soft loden fabrics meet white exposed concrete, illuminated by well-directed light. The house's own water source, geothermal energy, passive solar energy use and a photovoltaic system supply the house with energy what makes it self-sufficient. The windows are positioned in a way that there is no need for any shadowing elements at all. During winter, solar heat gain reduces costs and provides indoor climate comfort.

Exterior view chalet. Interior view.
Dining corner with panoramic window.
Chalet la Pedevilla with mountains.

Interior view living room.
View of the kitchen. Floor plan.

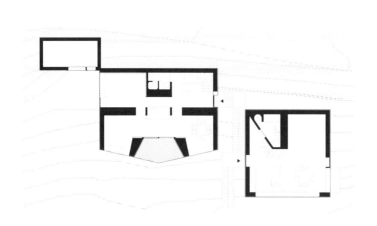

GETTING AROUND. THE DOLOMITES ARE WIDELY KNOWN AS THE UNIQUE MOUNTAIN LANDSCAPE OF SOUTH TYROL AND FOR THEIR EXTRAORDINARY SKI AREA AND OFFER A LOT OF VARIETY AT ANY TIME OF THE YEAR. THE TOWN OF BRUNECK AS THE MAIN DESTINATION OF THE PUSTO VALLEY AND ST. VIGILIO IN ENNEBERG, AS THE MAIN TOURISTIC SPOT OF THE GARDA VALLEY, GUARANTEES AN UNFORGETTABLE STAY. SOME OF THE HIGHLIGHTS ARE THE TWO LOCATIONS OF THE MESSNER MOUNTAIN MUSEUM IN RIPA AND CORONES (KRONPLATZ).

View of the house from below.
Interior view of the sleeping area.

INFORMATION. ARCHITECTS> GEBAUER.WEGERER.WITTMANN ARCHITEKTEN BDA // 2018. BOUTIQUE HOTEL> 3 GARDEN LOFTS OF 57, 58 AND 66 SQM // 4 GUESTS EACH // 1 BEDROOM AND A FOLDING DOUBLE BED IN THE LIVING ROOM // 1 BATHROOM. ADDRESS> GUNTRAMS 11, SCHWARZAU AM STEINFELD, AUSTRIA. WWW.GUNTRAMS11.AT

Garden lofts with views of the surrounding mountains. Living room with a floating folding double bed. Exterior view of the garden lofts with a fountain of petrified wood.

Gartenlofts Gut Guntrams

SCHWARZAU AM STEINFELD, AUSTRIA

The Guntrams estate's farm was joined by three new guesthouses with a restaurant and a store offering the farm's locally produced products. The new building with gastronomy and store was arranged along the road as a demarcation of the existing space and constitutes the backbone of the new facility. Facing the street, the building is very self-contained and clearly oriented to the beautiful orchards and crystal gardens. Due to limited space, the three new lofts had to be located directly in front of the utility and service building with its outdoor restaurant area.

Three wooden cubes were designed as hovering, irregularly shaped guesthouses, allowing the landscape below them to flow through, and to keep the view across the extensive orchards. On the one hand, this floating design creates a relationship between the restaurant area and the surrounding gardens, on the other hand, the higher position of the guest apartments offers a wonderful panoramic view of the Vienna Alps to the west.

Wood as the predominant building material was an obvious choice given the ecological and sustainable focus of the estate and the strong reference to the landscape. In addition, the sustainable choice of materials also creates a very gentle and natural connection between the new houses and the nature around them. Inside the garden lofts, the primary use of wood as construction material gives the guests also a sensorial experience of nature and allows them to enjoy an unforgettable stay.

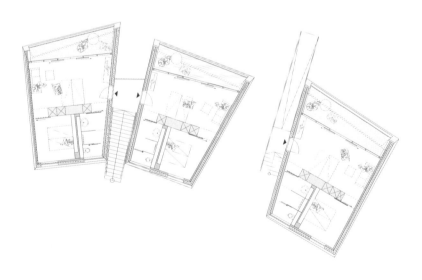

GETTING AROUND. THE BOUTIQUE HOTEL GUT GUNTRAMS IS LOCATED AT THE FOOT OF THE BUCKLIGE WELT HILLS, WITH A VIEW OF THE VIENNA ALPS. THIS IS A GREAT AREA FOR HIKING. THE CASTLE OF SEEBENSTEIN AND THE TÜRKENSTURZ CASTLE ARE WITHIN WALKING DISTANCE. THE THERMAL BATHS OF LINDBERG AND THE GOLF CLUBS OF LANDSBERG AND FÖHRENWALD ARE CLOSE BY. FOR THOSE WHO LOVE MOUNTAIN AIR THE SCHNEEBERG RAILWAY AND THE RAXSEILBAHN CABLEWAY WILL QUICKLY TAKE YOU UP. THERE ARE ALL KIND OF PLACES TO GO IN THE REGION LIKE DAY TRIPS TO THE WINE REGION OF LAKE NEUSIEDLERSEE OR TO VIENNA (60 KM).

Garden lofts at dusk. Floor plans.
Detail of the façade.

Interior view of the Marille garden loft
with loggia. View of a granite bathtub and vine.
The Veranda café and farm store.

INFORMATION. ARCHITECT>
BERNHARD STUCKY // 16TH CENTURY,
RESTORATION 2008. ALPINE BLOCK
CONSTRUCTION> 86 SQM //
4 GUESTS // 2 BEDROOMS //
1 BATHROOM. ADDRESS> EGGA 703,
BELLWALD, SWITZERLAND.
WWW.FERIENIMBAUDENKMAL.CH/
HUBERHAUS

Bedroom. Interior view. Exterior view in winter.
Panoramic view of the neighborhood.

Huberhaus

BELLWALD, SWITZERLAND

The Huberhaus in Bellwald, in the Upper Valais, is a typical alpine block house. It is located in the hamlet of Eggen, a few steps away from the village, and has a beautiful view. The year of construction of the historic house is unknown. The oldest parts of the building date back to the 16th century, according to research. In 1723 the house was rebuilt and restored. Mr. Klemenz Huber was the last inhabitant who lived in the house until 1891. He is the reason behind the name Huberhaus. Later owners used the house only as a storage place for tools and as a carpenter's workshop. From 1930 onwards, the house was empty and gradually fell into disrepair until it was taken over by the Holidays in Historical Buildings Foundation in 2006. In March 2008, after a two-year renovation phase that prioritized the preservation of the historic structure, the house was inaugurated. The stone plinth houses the cellar and on top of it is the wooden structure. The entrance connects directly with the kitchen in the rear part of the house, which is partly walled. The front part facing south contains the parlor and the bedroom above it. The northern part of the 18th-century Huber house was removed because of its poor condition, and a new wooden annex was built within the same structure, the roof was shingled. Today, this extension houses a new bathroom on the first floor and a second bedroom on the second floor. The Huber house was renovated in a most restrained way. Wherever possible, the existing structure was preserved and even enhanced.

Dining and living area.
View of the kitchen.

Exterior view in winter. Interior view.
Floor plans.

GETTING AROUND. BELLWALD IS A QUIET TOURIST DESTINATION, IDEAL FOR SUMMER AND WINTER BREAKS. IN SUMMER, HIKERS GET TO RICHENEN AND STEIBECHRIZ BY CHAIRLIFT, TAKING THEM TO A HIKING REGION WITH MOUNTAIN LAKES AND A PANORAMIC VIEW OF THE VALAISIAN MOUNTAIN WORLD. IN WINTER THE BELLWALD SKIING REGION ATTRACTS MAINLY SKIERS AND SNOWBOARDERS. IN THE FURTHER SURROUNDINGS THERE ARE ALL SORTS OF SIGHTS TO SEE, FOR EXAMPLE THE UNESCO WORLD HERITAGE SITE ALETSCH, THE BINN VALLEY OR THE GOMS REGION WITH ITS TRADITIONAL VILLAGES.

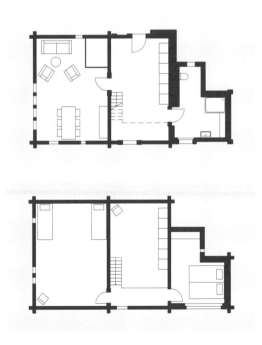

INFORMATION. ARCHITECT>
ERIK NISSEN JOHANSEN // 2018.
RESORT> CA. 5,750 SQM //
CA. 100 GUESTS // 47 BEDROOMS //
47 BATHROOMS. ADDRESS>
VIA NOVA 80, FLIMS, SWITZERLAND.
WWW.THEHIDEHOTELFLIMS.CH

The Hide

FLIMS, SWITZERLAND

The Hide is a cozy and comfortable place – with a very exquisite urban touch. It doesn't feel like a typical city hotel at all, though. The architecture and interior design are influenced by the alpine lifestyle and a modern alpine way of living. The hotel's interior design concept provides a beautiful, contemporary flair and its warm and welcoming atmosphere is also due to its fine lighting design. The designer team of Gothenburg-based studio Stylt Trampoli, known for its unusual and bold creations, displays its creative skills: extravagant and harmoniously coordinated color concepts, modern wallpaper and staged designer furniture invite guests to linger and relax inside.

The location at the heart of the recently opened Stenna complex is also quite unique. Various shopping facilities, a ski and bike rental, the ski and snowboard school, a cinema with four halls, a modern doctor's office and, last but not least, the Kindercity are just a short walk away without having to leave the building. The lower terminus of the mountain lift is just a few meters away and the ski slopes go right into the hotel's courtyard, right to the doorstep, so to speak. Therefore, in winter it's all about ski in, ski out!

Interior view. A private room. The bar area. Interior view of the common area with sofas.

Common area. Detail of the fireplace.
View of the restaurant. Floor plans.
Interior view room.

GETTING AROUND. IT COULDN'T BE MORE EASY, SKI IN, SKI OUT: STRAIGHT FROM THE HOTEL TO THE SLOPES (WWW.LAAX.COM). THERE IS A LARGE, ELEGANT SPA ON THE SECOND FLOOR WHICH IS A PERFECT PLACE TO RELAX. ON 1,000 SQM IT OFFERS THE MOST MODERN GYM EQUIPMENT, A FINNISH SAUNA WITH PANORAMIC VIEW OVERLOOKING THE MOUNTAINS, A STEAM BATH, SANARIUM, RAIN SHOWERS, A CHILL-OUT ROOM AS WELL AS A PRIVATE SPA AREA FOR TWO PEOPLE. THE HIDEAWAY CINEMA OFFERS ENTERTAINMENT IN SIX DIFFERENT CINEMA HALLS.

INFORMATION. ARCHITECT>
THOMAS FURTER // 2020.
TINY HOUSE> 25 SQM // 2 GUESTS //
1 BEDROOM // 1 BATHROOM.
ADDRESS> LARESCH 12, MATHON,
SWITZERLAND.
WWW.LARESCH.CH

Tiny House Laresch

MATHON, SWITZERLAND

The tiny house was designed as an extension to an existing mountain lodge. The building is located in the Swiss Alps at just under 1,600 meters above sea level. Sustainability was the top criterion during construction. The timber originates from the Beverin Nature Park, sheep's wool from Central European pastures, and the clay from the Jura Mountains. The building is heated using geothermal energy from the main house. The architecture of the building shows that it is possible to build a home in a small space with local and natural materials. Tiny House Laresch is a great example of how local wood can be used in nature-friendly construction.

The house has a living area with a dining area and a small kitchen. It is open to the roof and is fully glazed on the valley side. The sleeping area is on a gallery in the gable located above the bathroom. You have a great view of the mountain panorama from the bed. In fine weather, the terrace extends the room and becomes a kind of outdoor box seat with wonderful views.

Exterior view in winter. View of the living area. Detail of the dining area with view. Tiny house with snow.

Sleeping area with view. Detail of the bed.
Bathroom. Floor plan.

GETTING AROUND. THE BERGLODGE AND THE TINY HOUSE ARE LOCATED ON A SUNNY TERRACE IN THE MIDDLE OF THE SWISS ALPS NATURE PARK AT 1,600 M.A.S.L. THERE IS PEACE AND UNSPOILED NATURE AND AGAIN AND AGAIN YOU CAN ENJOY BREATHTAKING VIEWS OF THE MOUNTAINS. THE VIAMALA REGION OFFERS MANY OPPORTUNITIES FOR HIKING IN SUMMER. BESIDES THE FAMOUS VIAMALA GORGE, THERE ARE ALSO MANY OTHER ATTRACTIONS. IN WINTER YOU CAN EXPLORE THE AREA WITH SNOWSHOES, SLEDGES OR WALKING ON A WINTER HIKING TRAIL. THE THERMAL BATH IS NEARBY AND IS A GREAT PLACE TO RELAX.

Interior view tiny house.
Exterior view.

INFORMATION. ARCHITECTS>
OFIS ARCHITECTS AND AKT II, IN
COLLABORATION WITH STUDENTS
AT HARVARD UNIVERSITY GRADUATE
SCHOOL OF DESIGN, FREEAPPROVED
AND PD LJUBLJANA MATICA // 2015.
SHELTER> 12 SQM // 8 GUESTS.
ADDRESS> MOUNTAIN SKUTA,
ZGORNJE JEZERSKO, SLOVENIA.
WWW.PD-LJMATICA.SI/KOCE/
BIVAK-POD-SKUTO/

*View from the panoramic window. Alpine Shelter
Skuta surrounded by mountains. Side view.*

Exterior view. View into the wooden interior. Frontal view.

Alpine Shelter Skuta

MOUNTAIN SKUTA, SLOVENIA

The project was developed from an architectural design studio at the Harvard Graduate School of Design led by Rok Oman and Spela Videcnik from OFIS. In 2014, 13 students were asked to design an innovative yet practical shelter to meet the needs of the extreme alpine climate. Inspired by the vernacular architecture of Slovenia with its rich and diverse architectural heritage, the students developed 12 different designs. The challenge of the project were the forces of nature, extreme temperature fluctuations, impassable terrain at high altitude, difficult transport conditions and a respectful approach to nature.

It was finally the design of the students Frederick Kim, Katie MacDonald and Erin Pellegrino that convinced the jury because of its traditional alpine

architecture, the formality, and the chosen materiality. The project further was elaborated by OFIS architects and civil engineers from AKT II, assisted by mountaineers Anze Cokl, Milan Sorc and other engineers. The outer form and choice of materials of the bivouac respond to the extreme alpine conditions, and still allow views of the breathtaking landscape.

The house consists of three modules, divided to suit transport conditions, and also to divide the interior space. The design of the interior radiates both simplicity and functionality and can accommodate up to eight mountaineers.

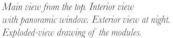

*Main view from the top. Interior view
with panoramic window. Exterior view at night.
Exploded-view drawing of the modules.*

GETTING AROUND. A DESTINATION FOR HIKERS AND CLIMBERS IN ALL SEASONS, THE SITE WITH THE EXISTING SHELTER IS LOCATED UNDER THE SKUTA MOUNTAIN IN KAMNIŠKE ALPE, SLOVENIA AT AN ELEVATION OF 2,070 M. IT SITS ALONG AN UNMARKED TRAIL LEADING TO THE SUMMIT OF SKUTA WITH AN ALTITUDE OF 2,532 M. EACH YEAR A FEW HUNDRED MOUNTAINEERS AND HIKERS STOP AT THE SHELTER, SOME FOR THE NIGHT, SOME ONLY FOR A BRIEF BREAK. THE SITE IS VALUED FOR ITS SPECTACULAR VIEWS.

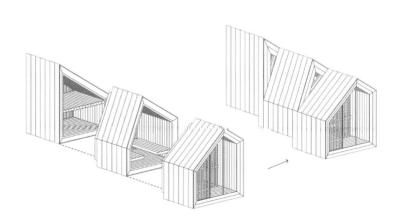

INFORMATION. ARCHITECTS>
TARA ARCHITEKTEN – HEIKE POHL
AND ANDREAS ZANIER // 2019.
HOTEL> 5,500 SQM // 84 GUESTS //
56 BEDROOMS // 56 BATHROOMS.
ADDRESS> FREIGASSE 8, JENESIEN,
BOLZANO, ITALY.
WWW.HOTEL-SALTUS.COM

Exterior view. Detail of the sauna.
Pool with panoramic view.

A bedroom. Interior view of the coffee shop area.

Eco Hotel Saltus

BOLZANO, ITALY

Take a breath, relax, enjoy the forest, and feel grounded – this is what the new Saltus Hotel in San Genesio Altesino near Bolzano was designed for. Every single choice of material, every single design solution was based on this concept. The three building units are situated at different heights on a steeply sloping hillside. A few incisions were made in these clearly defined structures, which interact with the striking terrain to create unique outside spaces such as terraces, sunbathing zones and balconies. Each room, each space is aligned with nature as a counterpart.

The towering and densely grown pine trees feel very close looking from one of the rooms. It is the huge Dolomites massif that attracts the eye from the lobby and the Sky Pool, while the eyes get lost in the blue of the sky. The skin is made of vertical, pre-grayed native larch, and it is cement-plastered surfaces and walnut elements that shape the interior. While the rooms look like a peek-a-boo towards the forest, opening up out of the glass front, the corridors almost hide everything that is outside. Moreover, there are many things that do not exist in the hotel: televisions in the rooms, pictures on the walls, playground attractions in the pool. This gives room for thought, for dreamy hours on the daybed by the window, and for getting lost in the blue of the sky above the water of the same color.

Interior view. Room with large window. Common living area with panoramic window.

Eco Hotel Saltus from the outside.
Interior view corridor.

GETTING AROUND. THE HIGH PLATEAU OF THE SALTEN WITH ITS EXTENSIVE HIKING POSSIBILITIES IS RIGHT ON THE DOORSTEP. VANTAGE POINTS, POWER SPOTS AND ALPINE INNS ARE READY TO BE DISCOVERED: YOUR FRIENDS AND FAMILY IN THIS SUNNY REGION ARE HORSES, CHESTNUT TREES AND LARCH FORESTS. THE CITY OF BOLZANO IS ONLY EIGHT MINUTES AWAY BY CABLE CAR. THIS IS A VERY ROMANTIC PLACE THAT ALSO OFFERS SHOPPING OPPORTUNITIES AND CULTURAL ACTIVITIES. NO MATTER WHETHER IT IS THE ALLEYS OF THE OLD TOWN, THE OETZI MUSEUM OR THE BOZEN CHRISTMAS MARKET, THERE IS ALWAYS SOMETHING FOR EVERYONE.

INFORMATION. ARCHITECTS>
GRÜNECKER & REICHELT
ARCHITEKTEN // 2018. TOWER
HOUSE> CA. 400 SQM // 8 GUESTS //
5 BEDROOMS // 3 BATHROOMS.
ADDRESS> GERLOSBERG 17 G,
ZELL AM ZILLER, AUSTRIA.
WWW.HOLZRAUSCH.DE

Turmhaus
Tirol

ZELL AM ZILLER, AUSTRIA

Turmhaus Tirol is located near
Zell am Ziller at an altitude of 1,261
meters at the entrance to the Austrian
Gerlostal valley in the community
of Gerlosberg. It is a joint project of
Grünecker & Reichelt and holzrausch.
The architectural and interior design
concept was developed over a period
of several years and then realized by
holzrausch and other selected partners
in close cooperation. Both cooperation
partners share a fascination for the
way materials and details have an
emotional impact, a minimalist and
timeless design language, and aim to
realize projects at the highest level of
craftsmanship. Turmhaus Tirol reflects
this shared vision in the contrasting yet
well-balanced combination of interior
and exterior spaces.

The building takes its cue from the
local architectural style, adopting and
reinterpreting characteristic features of
the neighboring farms, such as the
arrangement of windows according
to spatial function, a gable roof,
and a sunbaked façade. The steep
sloping terrain and the request to
make the house resemble the design
of a tower house gave rise to a
footprint of 8 x 8 meters. The tower
house extends over six levels. Its
foundation consists of three basement
levels. On top there are three more
floors with living, dining and sleeping
areas in timber construction.

Kitchen with balcony. Interior view.
Bathroom. Dining area with panoramic window.

A bedroom. Detail.
Longitudinal section.

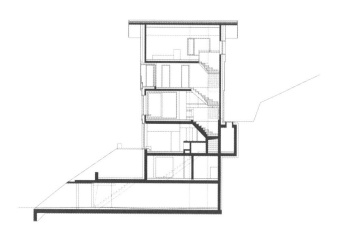

GETTING AROUND. MOUNT GERLOS, WHICH IS MAINLY POPULATED BY LOCALS, OFFERS THE IDEAL LOCATION NEXT TO THE LIVELY ZILLER VALLEY TO IMMERSE YOURSELF IN THE FASCINATING WORLD OF THE ZILLER VALLEY AND THE TUX ALPS IN SUMMER AS WELL AS IN WINTER. SITUATED AMIDST THE BEAUTIFUL MOUNTAIN LANDSCAPE, THE HOUSE IS THE PERFECT STARTING POINT TO EXPLORE NUMEROUS OUTDOOR ACTIVITIES (MOUNTAIN BIKING, HIKING, CLIMBING, RAFTING, SKIING) IN AND AROUND THE ZILLERTAL VALLEY.

Tower house Tirol with mountains.
Living area with fireplace.

INFORMATION. ARCHITECTS>
BRÜDERL ARCHITEKTUR GMBH
// 2019. APARTMENT> 62 SQM //
2 + 2 GUESTS // 1 BEDROOM //
1 BATHROOM. ADDRESS> PIRACH 11,
TROSTBERG, GERMANY.
WWW.WASSERTURM-PIRACH.DE

*Living room with panoramic view. Interior view
of the kitchen and dining area. A bedroom.
Exterior view of Pirach water tower.*

Wasserturm Pirach

TROSTBERG,
GERMANY

It is an extraordinary experience to take a break in the "Schorsch" lodging in the Pirach water tower near Trostberg. This monument, which is almost 30 meters high and characterizes the region between Lake Chiemsee and Lake Waginger in the Upper Bavarian foothills of the Alps, tells an exciting story. About 60 years after it was first put into operation, the water tower underwent extensive general renovation following its acquisition by the Brüderl family. The striking architectural jewel still keeps traces of its former use, but combines it with sophisticated designs, custom-made furniture design from Brüderl's in-house manufactory and exclusive living comfort.

The apartment's 69-square-meter living and dining area with kitchen, a bedroom and bathroom are integrated into the roundings of the tower's second floor. The panoramic window offers a unique view of the peaks of the Chiemgau Alps. Clever integration of technical relics into the modern interior design establishes a source of energy with an atmosphere that makes the vacation memories last for a long time.

Bedroom from the top. Detail of the panoramic window. Detail of the façade. Floor plan.

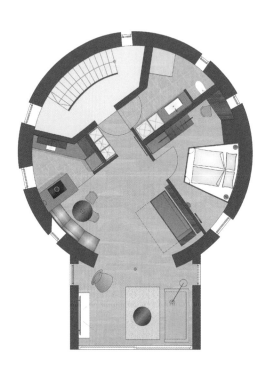

GETTING AROUND. IN THE IMMEDIATE VICINITY YOU WILL FIND THE CHIEMGAU MOUNTAINS WITH NUMEROUS HIKING POSSIBILITIES, GOLF COURSES, AMUSEMENT PARKS AND LAKES. ACTIVITIES: LAKE CHIEMSEE, DAY TRIPS TO SALZBURG (50 KM) AND MUNICH (100 KM), BAD REICHENHALL, BERCHTESGADEN AND THE KÖNIGSSEE, OUTDOOR ADVENTURE POOLS AND NUMEROUS LAKES FOR SWIMMING. ALSO IN WINTER THE REGION OFFERS MANY ACTIVITIES NEXT DOOR LIKE HIKING TOURS, CROSS-COUNTRY SKIING TRACKS IN CLASSIC AND SKATING STYLE, THE SKIING AREA AT THE HOCHFELLN, THE SKIING AREA WINKELMOOSALM, THE ICE-SKATING RINKS INZELL AND RUHPOLDING.

Living room.
Interior view.

INFORMATION. ARCHITECTS>
CHESEAUXREY ASSOCIÉS SA // 2016.
MOUNTAIN HUTS> MAYEN OLIVIER
50 SQM, MAYEN ETIENNE 58 SQM,
MAYEN JEAN 67 SQM, MAYEN
MADELEINE 98 SQM, MAYEN JOSEPH
118 SQM, MAYEN HENRI 19 SQM //
2–12 GUESTS // 1–3 BEDROOMS //
1–2 BATHROOMS. ADDRESS>
CHEMIN DES CEINTRES 12,
LA FORCLAZ, SWITZERLAND.
WWW.ANAKOLODGE.CH

Anakolodge

LA FORCLAZ, SWITZERLAND

Ruins of six agricultural buildings in the Val d'Hérens were saved from demolition and rebuilt respecting the traditional architecture of the Valais. Originally, these buildings were used to store supplies, and the stables for the Eringer cows were located just below the floor. The construction consisted of larch planks, which, depending on the building type, stood on wooden posts and granite stones that were used to protect from mice, or were placed on top of the dry-stone wall stables. In the so called raccards the families stored grain, hay, and other supplies. The barns were used to store the hay that was used to feed the cattle in winter. The granaries, located in the center of the village, were used to store provisions for the whole family.

The architect Olivier Cheseaux has succeeded in renovating the agricultural buildings, because on the one hand, a new use become possible, and on the other hand preserving the rough and at the same time delicate look of these houses that fit perfectly into the wild nature. Those Maiensässe, small huts, are fully equipped and heated to 20-21 degrees depending on the season. The consistently designed interiors, mostly made of simple materials, create a special atmosphere even in the smallest of spaces. The kitchen is fully equipped. The Anakolodge collaborates with the village store and the restaurants of the valley, doing justice to its concept based on respect, trust and love of nature and beauty.

Night view in winter. Detail of the entrance. Terrace with mountain view. General view.

51

A bedroom with large window. View of the balcony.
Sections of the cabins.

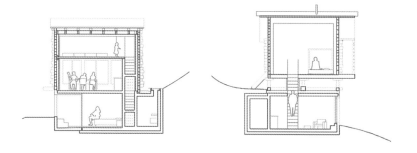

GETTING AROUND. OUTDOOR ACTIVITIES IN THE COUNTRYSIDE RANGE FROM HIKING TO FLYING, SKIING, PICKING PLANTS, TASTING, MEDITATING AND MARVELING. HOWEVER, THERE IS ALSO THE POSSIBILITY OF PERSONALIZED ACTIVITIES.

Exterior view of the garden.
Interior view of the living area.

INFORMATION. ARCHITECTS>
BERGMEISTERWOLF // 2017.
HOTEL> 3,220 SQM // 36 GUESTS //
18 BEDROOMS WITH BATHROOMS.
ADDRESS> VIA BRANDIS 2A,
LANA, ITALY.
WWW.BALLGUTHOF.COM/IT

Interior view of one room. Façade detail.
Exterior view from the vineyard.

Hotel Ballguthof

LANA, ITALY

The Boutique Hotel Ballguthof in the immediate vicinity of the golf course of Lana is surrounded by its own vineyards and a large park. The architect couple bergmeisterwolf realized this unique project in 2017 in collaboration with the artist Manfred Alois Mayr.

The Ballguthof combines rustic South Tyrolean tradition with modern innovative design. It consists of two connected buildings – a boutique hotel and a main house. It is amazing how the sloping roof surfaces merge, on the one hand, with the surrounding roofscape and, on the other hand, reinforced by the dark color scheme, with the mountain panorama. The new architecture goes hand in hand with the landscape: the rooftops play with the mountains behind them, while the black color of the concrete merges with that of the mountains reflecting in the windows and in the summer contrasts them. The interior of the new rooms, the parlors establish a kind of dialectical relationship with the past, now fulfilling some new functions, such as those of the bathroom, the kitchen or simply remaining a parlor.

The link between the landscape and the built space becomes more intense due to the green roofs and their planting. The loggias and terraces reinforce the play of contrasts and provide at the same time intimate and private areas. The curved lines of the roofs are echoed in the balcony railings, which have changing layouts. The dynamically designed façade thus manages to constantly tell new stories and create new characters, depending on the perspective.

GETTING AROUND. LANA, MERANO AND ITS SURROUNDINGS OFFER WONDERFUL OPPORTUNITIES FOR RELAXATION AND ACTIVITIES, SUCH AS GOLF, HORSEBACK RIDING, NORDIC WALKING, MOUNTAIN BIKING OR TENNIS IN CHARMING NATURAL SURROUNDINGS. THERE IS ALSO A RICH CULTURAL OFFER IN THE CITY OF MERANO, WHICH BELONGS TO THE PROVINCE OF SOUTH TYROL AND IS ONLY ABOUT 12 KM AWAY AND IS KNOWN FOR ITS SPAS AND ART NOUVEAU-STYLE BUILDINGS.

Frontal view. Floor plans. Exterior detail of the modern architecture of the building.

Interior view. View of the bar area. Façade with parapet details.

INFORMATION. ARCHITECT>
MARX / LADURNER // 2013.
HOTEL> CA. 6,500 SQM // 90 GUESTS //
46 BEDROOMS // 46 BATHROOMS.
ADDRESS> BURGEIS 82, MALS, ITALY.
WWW.WEISSESKREUZ.IT

Hotel Weisses Kreuz

MALS, ITALY

Sometimes you might think that in the village of Burgusio (Burgesi) time stands still. It is quiet place. You won't find any hustle and bustle in the alleys of this South Tyrolean village. Nevertheless, the people of Burgusio are not from yesterday. They appreciate both past as well as new things. This is especially the case of the Theiner family. It all started with a village store. Over the decades, the Weisse Kreuz developed into what it is today. Thanks to vision, courage, and entrepreneurial spirit. The Weisse Kreuz consists of three independent buildings that connect by the small village square. The whitewashed main building gives the hotel its name. Just a few steps away, another gateway to the past opens. The Ansitz zum Löwen is a place that makes every architecturally inclined heart skip a beat. This is where modern exposed concrete snuggles up to 800-year-old walls. Accurately placed glass surfaces merge with fine Renaissance carvings in a delicate symbiosis. The Theiner family, in collaboration with the South Tyrolean architect duo Marx/Ladurner, has gently awakened the estate from its slumber. Guests will hardly be able to get out of their amazement. Where else could you rest in the former princely ballroom or take a bath in a former smokehouse? As all good things come in threes: the modern new building is an absolute delight. It is characterized by straight lines, restrained design and open architecture that invite visitors to let your gaze wander.

Interior view of a room. Detail of the sauna. Interior view of the Weisses Kreuz. Front view of the building.

Exterior view of the façade. Detail of a bedroom with large window. View of the bathroom. Floor plan.

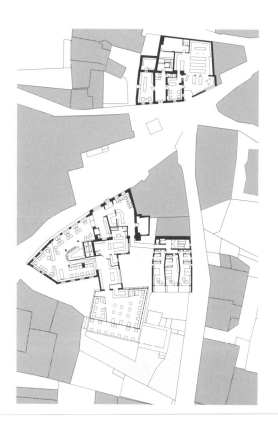

GETTING AROUND. HUNDREDS OF YEARS OLD IRRIGATION CHANNELS, NUMEROUS HIKING TRAILS AND A DENSE NETWORK OF MOUNTAIN BIKE TRAILS WIND THEIR WAY THROUGH THE RICH CULTURAL LANDSCAPE. ON THEIR VACATION IN VINSCHGAU IN SOUTH TYROL, SKIERS WILL FIND FIVE SUN-DRENCHED SKI AREAS, HIKERS WILL DISCOVER THE VINSCHGER HÖHENWEG AND BE TEMPTED BY THE 3,000-METER PEAKS HIGH UP IN THE AIR. TODAY, THE ROMAN ROAD VIA CLAUDIA AUGUSTA ENJOYS NEW ATTENTION AMONG CYCLISTS: AN 80 KM LONG, EASY-TO-MASTER BIKE PATH STRETCHES FROM MALS TO MERANO PASSING HISTORIC CHURCHES, CASTLES, RUINS AS WELL AS ANCIENT SITES IN THE VINSCHGAU VALLEY.

A bedroom of the Weisses Kreuz.
Common relaxation area.

INFORMATION. ARCHITECTS> NOA* NETWORK OF ARCHITECTURE // 2020. HOTEL> 38 SQM PER SUITE // 20 GUESTS // 10 SUITES // 10 BATHROOMS. ADDRESS> HENRIK-IBSENSTRASSE 17, SIUSI, ITALY. FLORIS.HOTELFLORIAN.IT

Room with a large panoramic window. View of the bathroom. Exterior view from the garden. View of the main façade.

Floris Green Suites

SIUSI, ITALY

Sunlight fills the room. The modern design is characterized by its natural style. The Floris Green Suites is surrounded by the captivating mountain scenery, where luxury and privacy blend into a perfect feeling of well-being. Located on the idyllic outskirts of Siusi allo Sciliar in South Tyrol, these ten exclusive suites radiate a lightness of being through their modern architecture. The independent structure blends perfectly into the magnificent park with its cozy oases of tranquility, the outdoor pool and the mighty trees.

The challenge of setting the chalets apart from the actual terrain, thus leaving the charming hotel park in its full glory, has been completely successful. The self-contained "tree houses" are perched on three-meter-high supports and provide a wonderful view of the park. In order to make the architectural ensemble look dynamic and to create the effect of a naturally grown structure, the houses were slightly offset.

The interior is dominated by a muted green interspersed with gray tones, completing the peaceful tree house feeling. The Floris Green Suites is a natural hideaway with endless horizons, openness, personal freedom and pure wellness thanks to a private balcony with bathtub, private sauna and selected natural materials that proves: where architecture embraces the diversity of nature, it is never perceived as a foreign body.

Detail of the façade. Front view of the building. The swimming pool from the top. Detail of the façade.

GETTING AROUND. A SKI PARADISE IN WINTER, AND A SOURCE OF POWER FOR HIKERS IN SUMMER – THE NATURE AROUND THE ALPE DI SIUSI IS UNIQUE. WIDE ALPINE MEADOWS AND DEEP FORESTS SPREAD OUT IN FRONT OF THE MIGHTY SCILIAR, WHICH BEARS WITNESS TO THE MILLIONS OF YEARS OF HISTORY OF THE DOLOMITES. THE PICTURESQUE OLD TOWNS OF BOLZANO OR BRESSANONE ARE A MUST FOR CULTURE ENTHUSIASTS, WHILE GOURMETS CAN ENJOY THE UNIQUE SYMBIOSIS OF ALPINE AND MEDITERRANEAN FLAVORS.

INFORMATION. ARCHITECT> IKE IKRATH // 1924, CONTINUOUSLY DEVELOPED. HOTEL> 70 GUESTS + KIDS // 29 ROOMS + BAR, LOUNGE, RESTAURANT, KIDS CLUB, SPA. ADDRESS> KAISERHOFSTRASSE 14, BAD GASTEIN, AUSTRIA. WWW.HAUS-HIRT.COM

Living area with mountain view. Interior view living room. Interior view restaurant.

Alpine Spa Hotel Haus Hirt

BAD GASTEIN, AUSTRIA

Authentically alpine but with a designer's eye, Haus Hirt welcomes guests and lovers of modern and eclectic design. Full of activities for the body and soul, the hotel features nine suites and twenty rooms, each offering a unique atmosphere and individual layout. Designed by Ike Ikrath and Elma Choung with lighting by Viennese designer Megumi Ito, the hotel's attention to detail is undeniable and inspiring. Lovingly styled with natural materials, Haus Hirt has always been a retreat for reset and reflection alike, offering a sparkly space for friends and families, for writers and artists, for the old and young. Built in the 1920s as a basecamp for urban adventurers, Haus Hirt has been continuously refreshed, updated, and cared for over the years. Today, it still calls to the free-spirits and mountain enthusiasts, boasting awe-inspiring views mixed with Belle Epoque glamour, and a creative twist on where modern meets retro.

Engaging and energized, Haus Hirt is inclusive and rejuvenating, even offering an on-property thermal spa with healing hot springs. Dedicated to the surrounding mountains and incredible landscape, the Ikraths have seamlessly translated their love of nature, art, literature and design into a beautiful experience, effortlessly sharing the greatest beauty of the region. Cheerful and inviting, Haus Hirt offers daily guided hikes, yoga and more for guests looking to escape the city.

GETTING AROUND. A PICTURESQUE HIDEAWAY IN THE AUSTRIAN ALPS, BAD GASTEIN EMBODIES THE FREE-THINKING, ART-DRIVEN AND DESIGN-FORWARD SPIRIT OF THE REGION. SURROUNDED BY SKI SLOPES, NATURE TRAILS, SWIMMING, HIKING, AND THERMAL BATHS, BAD GASTEIN IS AN OUTDOOR ENTHUSIAST'S DREAM. WITH WELLNESS AT THE FOREFRONT, THE AREA IS WELL-KNOWN FOR ITS TRANSFORMATIVE POWERS, INCREDIBLE HEALING PROPERTIES, UNIQUE ATMOSPHERE, AND INSPIRING SURROUNDINGS.

The complex and mountains.
Interior view. A detail of a bedroom.

Room with panoramic view. A bedroom.
Restaurant in the blue hour.

INFORMATION. ARCHITECTS>
DURISCH + NOLLI ARCHITETTI // 2019.
HOTEL> 2,100 SQM // 76 GUESTS //
16 BEDROOMS // 22 BATHROOMS.
ADDRESS> CAMPRA, TICINO,
SWITZERLAND.
WWW.CAMPRALODGE.CH

View of the spa area with wooden surfaces.
Interior view. Front view.

Exterior view in winter.
Interior view of a room.

Campra Alpine Lodge & Spa

TICINO, SWITZERLAND

Nestled in a wonderful landscape with typical Nordic features, the Nordic Campra Ski Center is a perfectly equipped facility for cross-country skiing in the Swiss Alps. The natural slope of the terrain is broken up by the concrete base of the building, which contains all the services and infrastructures available to all athletes.

The base rises from the ground to form the large terrace of the restaurant with a sloping staircase that provides direct access to the parking lot and divides the structured main entrance. The wooden structure on the concrete base which includes the reception on the ground floor, the bar, the kitchen and two restaurants and dining rooms that are flexible in size due to modular and movable walls transforming them into a large room for special events. All rooms on the second floor are designed according to a regular and precise module that optimizes the management of the different types of utilities. The head of the building is strengthened in its expression towards Lucomagno Street by an additional floor that houses the spa. The use of wood as a building material guarantees excellent environmental and energy characteristics and improves the overall sustainability of the new settlement.

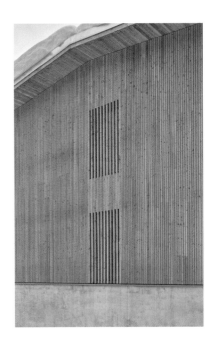

Lodge with mountains. Interior view of a room.
Detail of the wooden façade. Floor plans.

GETTING AROUND. CAMPRA ALPINE LODGE & SPA IS THE IDEAL ACCOMMODATION FOR EVERYONE WHO IS PASSIONATE ABOUT NATURE AND OUTDOOR ACTIVITIES. IN WINTER GUESTS CAN ENJOY THE 30 KM OF CROSS-COUNTRY SKI TRAILS, AN ICE-SKATING CIRCUIT AS WELL AS FOREST TRAILS. IN SUMMER THERE ARE MANY EXCURSION POSSIBILITIES BY MTB OR ON FOOT. FOR THOSE WHO LIKE TO RELAX, THE SPA OF THE HOTEL IS OPEN ALL YEAR ROUND.

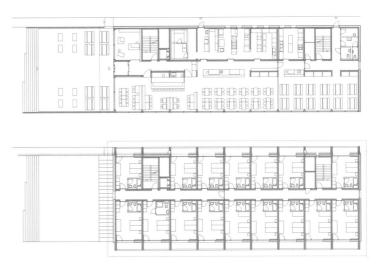

INFORMATION. ARCHITECTS>
RURALURBAN // 2018.
FARMHOUSE> 275 SQM // 10 GUESTS
// 5 BEDROOMS // 3 BATHROOMS.
ADDRESS> OBERSTEINERWEG 5,
KLOBENSTEIN, RENON, ITALY.
WWW.OBERSTEINERHOF.IT

*View of the kitchen island. Interior view.
Kitchen and dining area. Living room
with large windows.*

Obersteinerhof

RENON, ITALY

The 600-year-old walls of the Obersteinerhof on the Renon plateau tell new stories since 2017, because there was paid great attention to achieve a balance between tradition and innovation during the construction of the extension and its restoration: a fresh alpine design made its way into the historic walls. All rooms got a makeover, and the apartments were designed with careful attention to detail, in order to give each apartment its own conceptual and aesthetic identity. The sophisticated and comfortable interior is the result of large French doors and the special choice of furnishing elements, both functional and flooded with light, in dialogue with the idyllic nature around.

The apartment "Wald" has two floors. In the basement there is a large open space with a eat-in kitchen that is flooded with light. The natural color of wood sets the tone and is highlighted by contrasting bluish elements of the furnishing. The room's protagonist is a large table with an integrated kitchen island. On the second floor are the bedrooms, which have a warm and cozy feel.

The apartment "Acker" is characterized by its new and contemporary look. The bedrooms and living area on the first floor are particularly cozy. A minimalist wooden staircase connects to the lower floor, that has a large eat-in kitchen and the bathroom. This room is just amazing with its tiles made of red porphyry from Montiggl and a bathtub with spectacular views of the impressive alpine scenery.

Dining area. Bathroom overlooking the living room.

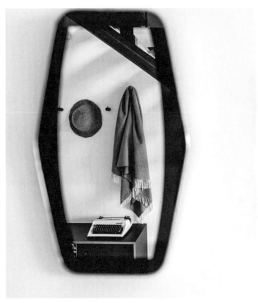

Interior view of kitchen.
Detail. A bedroom.

GETTING AROUND. THE RENON
(RITTEN) CABLE CAR TAKES GUESTS
UP IN JUST A FEW MINUTES. RIGHT
THERE IS A BEAUTIFUL AND RELAXING
HOLIDAY AREA. TO BE MORE PRECISE,
THE RITTEN STRETCHES FROM THE
VINEYARD SLOPES NEAR BOLZANO
AT AROUND 300 M ABOVE SEA LEVEL
ALL THE WAY UP TO MOUNT RENON
AT 2,260 M ABOVE SEA LEVEL! THE
REGION OFFERS AN EXCEPTIONALLY
DIVERSE VEGETATION, 15 CHAR-
ISMATIC LOCATIONS AND PLENTY
OF HIGHLIGHTS TO DISCOVER:
THE EARTH PYRAMIDS, THE VILLAGE
OF LONGOMOSSO, THE BEES
MUSEUM IN COSTOLOVARA, LAKE
COSTOLOVARA (WOLFSGRUBNER
SEE) AND THE RENON TRAIN
(RITTNER BAHNL) ARE ONLY
SOME OF THEM.

INFORMATION. ARCHITECTS>
EN.AR[TEC] // 2015.
APARTMENTS> 700 SQM // 16 GUESTS
// 8 BEDROOMS // 8 BATHROOMS.
ADDRESS> HERZOG-DIET-STRASSE 1,
BRUNICO, ITALY.
WWW.NMHOF.IT

Niedermairhof

BRUNICO, ITALY

The Niedermairhof, whose foundation walls date back to the 14th century is in Dietenheim, on the outskirts of the town of Brunico. The farm was recently in a structurally poor condition. The Mayr family has decided to give new life to the building and to renovate the house from the ground up. The three upper floors were almost completely gutted, and the historic collar beam roof truss was preserved. The ceilings are a composite wood-concrete construction, and the façade and windows were renovated in accordance with historic preservation standards.

On the site of the former outside toilet, a contemporary annex was built, which stands out from the residential building and at the same time blends into the courtyard ensemble. The façade was made of blackened sheet steel, which matches the historic surroundings with its lively color shades and thus reduces the force of the crystalline design of the annex. The eight suites have been individually furnished with great attention to detail and have barrier-free access. One of the suites and the reception area were designed by artist Ingrid Canins. She also hand-painted her own motifs to complement the wallpaper paintings in the large hallway. The interior concept juxtaposes the existing historic furniture with classic designer furniture; the whole design is based on a dialogue between ancient walls and contemporary design.

Exterior view of the ensemble of buildings. Staircase. Interior view of a bedroom. Front view.

Niedermairhof from below. Entrance with stairs.
Detail. Floor plan. Detail of the exterior.

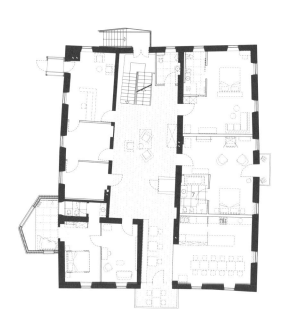

GETTING AROUND. DIETENHEIM IS A CITY DISTRICT OF BRUNICO IN THE PUSTERIA VALLEY. THERE IS THE CORONES, THE LARGEST SKIING AREA IN SOUTH TYROL WITH 119 KM OF PISTES AND 32 LIFTS AND OTHER FACILITIES TO GET UP TO SKI. IN THE EAST YOU CAN SEE THE PEAKS OF THE PRAGS DOLOMITES, THEY ARE PART OF THE UNESCO WORLD CULTURAL HERITAGE. IN SUMMER THERE ARE SEVERAL WATERFALLS TO EXPLORE: THE KNEIPP PATH IN RISCONE, THE RIENZA GORGE IN BRUNICO AND THE REINBACH WATERFALLS IN SAND IN TAUFERS. THE ANTHOLZ LAKE, THE TOBLACH LAKE AND OF COURSE THE BRAIES LAKE ARE WORTH A VISIT. THE FOLKLORE MUSEUM OF DIETENHEIM WITH ITS CENTURIES-OLD BUILDINGS IS LOCATED RIGHT NEXT TO THE ACCOMMODATION. THE MESSNER MOUNTAIN MUSEUMS RIPA (BRUNICO) & CORONES (KRONPLATZ) ARE ARCHITECTURAL HIGHLIGHTS.

INFORMATION. ARCHITECTS>
VENTIRAARCHITEKTEN // 2006.
TERRACED HOUSES> 320 SQM //
4–8 GUESTS PER APARTMENT //
2–3 BEDROOMS // 2–3 BATHROOMS.
ADDRESS> SCHMIEDSEGG 661,
KAPPL, AUSTRIA.
WWW.ARADIRA.AT

Exterior view.
Detail of the exterior staircase.
Kitchen and living area.

Front view from the garden.
Terrace with panoramic view.
A bedroom.

Aradira Appartements

KAPPL, AUSTRIA

Many of the agricultural buildings and the names of the villages in Kappl still bear witness to their Rhaeto-Romanic origins. This is also the case of the name of the house Aradira, which is derived from the Rhaeto-Romanic name for potato field and mirrors the original use of the land lying on a steep slope.

The Aradira is located on the northern hillside of the village of Kappl and faces east and west. The building's ascending geometry is based on the slope's inclination, which is 13 meters long. The vehicle parking facilities, as well as private ski equipment and bicycle storage facilities are located at street level. The individual residences are accessed via the east-facing roofed open staircase. Since each of the four apartments has its own entrance door, there is a real feeling of spending holidays in a very private home.

On each apartment's entrance level there are two bedrooms with an additional sofa bed and a private bathroom. The second floor, accessed by a single flight of wooden stairs, offers an open view of the 3,000-meter peaks next door. On the first floor there is a living and kitchen area equipped with a tiled stove and a terrace to relax on. The sauna located in the northwest part of the apartments invite to recap the day's events.

The Aradira Appartements are completely made of wood, local slate and local larch wood cladding. Loden fabrics add colorful accents to each apartment and a heat pump with a geothermal probe is used for heating.

Interior view.
Townhouses at night. Barbecue area.
Kitchen and dining area.
Floor plans.

GETTING AROUND. BENEFIT FROM THE SKIING AREA OF KAPPL, ISCHGL, GALTÜR AND LAKE WITH OVER 300 KM OF SLOPES AND 55 CABLE CARS AND LIFTS IN WINTER. THERE ARE BEAUTIFUL CROSS-COUNTRY TRAILS BETWEEN ISCHGL AND GALTÜR OFFERING WONDERFUL PANORAMIC VIEWS, AND SOME WINTER HIKING TRAILS ALONG THE OLD VALLEY TRAIL AND THE SKI AREAS. IT'S ALL ABOUT BIKING IN SUMMER, AND THOSE WHO ARE EXPERIENCED CAN EXCERCISE WITHOUT ASSISTENCE AND THE OTHER ONES CAN GET SOME HELP. THE PROXIMITY TO THE HISTORIC OLD TOWN OF INNSBRUCK OR MERANO WILL MAKE EVERYONE'S STAY UNFORGETTABLE.

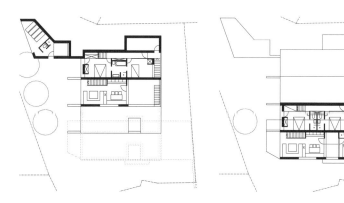

INFORMATION. ARCHITECT>
ELMAR UNTERHAUSER EU ARCHITECTS
// INTERIOR DESIGN> BIQUADRA
// 2019. SUITES> 510 SQM // 18–26
GUESTS // 9 BEDROOMS // 13
BATHROOMS. ADDRESS>
LAUBEN 309, MERANO, ITALY.
WWW.KUNTINOSUITES.COM

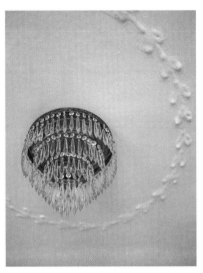

Living room. Detail of a chandelier.
Interior view of the suite.

Kuntino
Suites

MERANO, ITALY

During the renovation project, the historic Laubenhaus in Merano's Laubengasse was converted into nine spacious suites between 40 and 75 square meters on the two upper floors and Kuntino's Bar on the ground floor. The renovation of the building, under the direction of the local architect Elmar Unterhauser with his office EU Architects, and the interior design of the individual suites and the bar, under the direction of interior designer Christina Biasi-von Berg, with her office Biquadra, result in an attractive project, which on the one hand emphasizes the historical importance and character of the building, and at the same time provides the comfort and spatial generosity of contemporary living. The spatial structure was improved to suit the new use, and the highlighting of elements of historical importance,

for example the central staircase, give the building, which is significant in terms of architectural history, a fresh identity.

As a result, the historic charm that characterizes Merano is palpable in every suite, although each one is different from the others. Outside and inside, the traces of time remain visible, as new materials stand out from the pre-existing ones through their surface texture and color. Each of the nine suites is a carefully selected mix of locally found details and specially designed elements combined with luxurious furnishings to make it a special vacation home for design lovers, nostalgic people and discerning travelers.

GETTING AROUND. THE KUNTINO SUITES ARE LOCATED IN THE HEART OF MERANO'S OLD TOWN. LOCAL HISTORICAL BUILDINGS, MUSEUMS, STORES AND LOCAL BUSINESSES ARE ATTRACTIVE FOR CITY AND CULTURE ENTHUSIASTS. NUMEROUS HIKING TRAILS AND SKI AREAS IN THE SURROUNDINGS OFFER UNFORGETTABLE EXPERIENCES AND SCENERY FOR ACTIVE GUESTS. LET'S NOT TO MENTION THE CULINARY EXPERIENCES...

Exterior view. Floor plan.
Kitchen and dining area.

Common chill-out area.
Detail staircase. A bedroom.

INFORMATION. OWNERS>
SZILVIA AND REINHARD RAUTER //
2019. PAVILIONS> 120–140 SQM //
8–12 GUESTS // 4 BEDROOMS //
4 BATHROOMS. ADDRESS>
STILUMSERSTRASSE 4,
FELDTHURNS, ITALY.
WWW.DIETRICHHOF.COM

Dietrichhof — a bsunders Platzl

FELDTHURNS, ITALY

The Dietrichhof's comfort is based on sustainable and ecological construction. The old barn has four modern pavilions, which are assigned to the elements of earth, fire, water, and air. This is a place where you can breathe and relax in the truest sense of the word. The biodegradable building materials used include exclusively sustainable and natural materials such as straw, wood and clay. The excellent indoor climate is due to excellent insulating properties and moisture-regulating loam, which has a positive effect on the guests' well-being. The layout of the rooms is well designed, and together with its endless views into the vast nature this makes a stay at Dietrichhof unique.

The barrier-free pavilions are 30 and 37 square meters in size and can accommodate two to four people. They include a double bed, a dining and living area with sofa bed and a balcony overlooking the beautiful nature, the wonderful mountains.

View of the panoramic terrace. Interior view of one bedroom. Detail of the kitchen. Front view of the ensemble with mountain panorama.

Interior view of one pavilion. Detail of a common area. Small window with a view of the thatched walls. Front view.

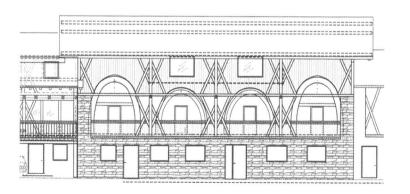

GETTING AROUND. GUESTS ENJOY ABSOLUTE RELAXATION AT THE HIGHEST LEVEL AWAY FROM THE VILLAGE AND HUSTLE AND BUSTLE. THE DIETRICHHOF IS LOCATED IN THE VILLAGE OF VELTURNO (FELDTHURNS), 1,187 M ABOVE SEA LEVEL, IN THE VALLE ISARCO LOW MOUNTAIN RANGE IN THE HEART OF SOUTH TYROL. SNOW-COVERED AND WILD AND ROMANTIC LANDSCAPES ARE A PARADISE FOR SKIERS AND SNOW LOVERS. THE MAGICAL LANDSCAPE WITH COLORFUL FLOWER MEADOWS, GIANT MOUNTAIN PEAKS AND FASCINATING VIEWS IS CHARACTERIZED BY SOFT PINK APPLE BLOSSOMS AND ITS UNIQUE SPRING AWAKENING – A PERFECT PLACE FOR ACTIVE HOLIDAYS AND PEOPLE SEEKING RELAXATION.

General view by night.
Detail of the structure.

INFORMATION. ARCHITECTS> NOA*
NETWORK OF ARCHITECTURE // 2020.
HOTEL> 2,890 SQM // 88 GUESTS //
44 BEDROOMS // 44 BATHROOMS.
ADDRESS> TORGGLERHOF 19, ST.
MARTIN IM PASSEIER, SALTAUS, ITALY.
WWW.APFELHOTEL.COM

Main view of the buildings from the garden.
Apfelhotel Torgglerhof. Interior view of a room.

Apfelhotel Torgglerhof

SALTAUS, ITALY

As they say in German, the apple doesn't fall far from the tree. The Apfelhotel in Saltaus in South Tyrol is breaking new ground with its new, young generation, but without completely abandoning the old paths. Studio noa* has turned a place that has grown historically into a home of senses and shared moments. Located in the heart of South Tyrol's cultural landscape, the Torgglerhof has its roots in classic apple growing, but has evolved over time into a welcoming place where people meet and enjoy.

The old barn next to the existing main house with restaurant was cored and transformed in 2016. The first floor behind the original façade is used to prepare delicacies made, among other things, from apples grown on the site. The guestrooms are located upstairs. The "Apple Sauna", the first part of a spacious wellness and recreation area, was built in parallel. There are also new suites that fit into the structure of the Haufenhof and have a rural look. This way, the character of the ensemble remains intact and keeps its dimensions.

The antithesis to this rural development is the green and modern garden architecture of the wellness area in the center of the whole site. The new garden suites, three independent buildings with a total of 18 guestrooms on three floors are located in the east. Their gable roofs echo the architectural language of the surrounding area and blend tradition and modernity through their façade design. Each of the 10 individually designed rooms and suites captivates with its high-quality architecture and provides a very special atmosphere.

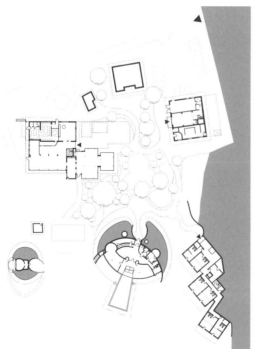

GETTING AROUND. THE RECENTLY OPENED SPA HAS AN "ADULTS ONLY" AREA ON THE UPPER FLOOR WITH A SAUNA LOUNGE, A RELAXATION ROOM, A FINNISH SAUNA, A STEAM BATH AND A TERRACE WITH AN OUTDOOR SHOWER. BUT AROUND THE APFELHOF THERE IS A LOT TO EXPLORE, TOO: THE MERANO COUNTRYSIDE OFFERS NOT ONLY CYCLISTS, GOLFERS AND EXPLORERS A WONDERFUL ENVIRONMENT, THERE ARE ALSO BEAUTIFUL PLACES TO GO IN THE CITY OF MERANO. THE HOSTS ALSO CAN HELP WITH INSIDER TIPS.

The wellness area, a "green heart".
Site plan. Relaxation area
with panoramic view.

Dining area from the garden. Wellness area.
Exterior view of Apfelhotel Torgglerhof.

INFORMATION. ARCHITECTS>
RLC ARCHITEKTEN, HERMANN AND
KATHARINA STUCKI SCHMEZER // 2013.
OLD FACTORY> LOFT SUITE 330 SQM
AND TOWER LOFT 90 SQM // 4 AND
8 GUESTS // 2 AND 4 BEDROOMS //
1 AND 2 BATHROOMS. ADDRESS>
ALTE SPINNEREI, MURG AM
WALENSEE, SWITZERLAND.
WWW.LOFTHOTEL.CH/UEBERNACH-
TEN/FERIENWOHNUNGEN/

*View of a loft suite's bedroom. Detail of a tower
loft's kitchen. Bathroom loft suite. Interior view
of the loft suite dining and living area.*

Lofthotel and Sagibeiz

MURG AM WALENSEE,
SWITZERLAND

The region is characterized by Lake Walen and the majestic mountains that resemble a fjord. The water of the lake is turquoise blue like the Caribbean. All of the 19 rooms at the Lofthotel and Sagibeiz reflect the region's industrial past and are named after a workroom at the old spinning mill in Murg.

The former tower with water for firefighting was converted into a five-story tower suite for a maximum of four people. The tower suite is equipped with a tea kitchen (two hotplates, small oven), a dining area, balcony, living room, one king-size bed, two single beds, shower/WC, WLAN, flat-screen TV, radio, an iPod docking station, a hairdryer, and a wonderful view of the mountains and Lake Walen. The balcony faces the inner courtyard. The 330-square-meter loft suite has four loft rooms (double rooms),

two bathrooms with shower/WC or bath/WC, a kitchen, a very spacious living area and a balcony located all on one level. It is fully equipped with a six-meter-long solid wood table, various seating areas, large flat-screen TV, radio, iPod docking station, hairdryer, WLAN and offers lake and mountain views as well. The largest chestnut forest north of the Alps behind the house inspired the interior design. In both units, individually designed unique pieces of chestnut wood were combined with designer furniture and artwork.

*Interior view of the loft suite's open-plan
living area. Bedroom tower loft.*

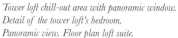

Tower loft chill-out area with panoramic window.
Detail of the tower loft's bedroom.
Panoramic view. Floor plan loft suite.

GETTING AROUND. WATER SPORTS AND NATURE ARE POPULAR DURING THE SUMMER AND AUTUMN, IN THE WINTER SNOW SPORTS, AND IN THE SPRING SOMETIMES ALL OF IT TOGETHER. MOREOVER, THERE ARE ART EXHIBITIONS TO VISIT. ZURICH IS A 45-MINUTE DRIVE AWAY, AND IT TAKES 25 MINUTES TO GET TO BAD RAGAZ. TRIPS TO CHUR, GLARUS, NÄFELS AND VADUZ ARE HIGHLY RECOMMENDED. THERE ARE A LOT OF PLACES TO DISCOVER AROUND THE LAKE: CAR-FREE QUINTEN, TOBOGGANING, CLIMBING AND HIKING ON THE FLUMSERBERG IN SUMMER, SKIING AND OTHER WINTER SPORTS IN WINTER.

INFORMATION. ARCHITECT>
FLORIAN NAGLER // 2012.
NATURE HOTEL & HEALTH
RESORT> 9–36 SQM PER ROOM //
100 GUESTS // 60 BEDROOMS //
60 BATHROOMS. ADDRESS>
TANNERHOFSTRASSE 32,
BAYRISCHZELL, GERMANY.
WWW.TANNERHOF.DE

Tannerhof

BAYRISCHZELL, GERMANY

A down-to-earth, relaxed atmosphere, the coexistence of young and old, of sound and silence, of spirits and herbal tea. The accommodation oscillates between hotel, health, organic gourmet cuisine, culture, and nature. It is ambiguous, artistic, loving. To spend vacations at the Tannerhof is great for both the mind and the body. It offers therapeutic fasting as well as a five-course slow food menu and rooms from 9 to 36 square meters. For once, the Tannerhof's architecture and philosophy are strict in this regard: chacun à sa façon. What sounds like a cliché makes the Tannerhof an inspiring place – it is avantgarde in its authenticity. On the one hand simple, almost naive, lovingly quirky, and digitally slowed down. Design comes from the heart and not from the PC. However, architect Florian Nagler introduced modernity at its best: cautious respect for the existing buildings that have grown over generations. The subtle, elegant architectural framing of buildings from different eras even reinforce the heart of the building – the venerable farming house Alte Tann. Both of Nagler's hut towers from 2012 are contemporary neighbors next to hermit's huts from 1905 and they are complementary, not dominant. The architectural coexistence outdoors joins the Tannerhof philosophy indoors.

Interior view of Almzimmer. Hut tower and surroundings. Façade. General view of the Tannerhof.

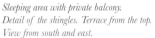
Sleeping area with private balcony.
Detail of the shingles. Terrace from the top.
View from south and east.

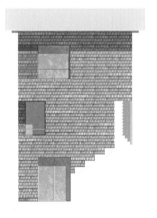

GETTING AROUND. THE TANNERHOF IS NESTLED ON A SLOPE ABOVE BAYRISCHZELL – WITH A VIEW ON THE WENDELSTEIN MOUNTAIN AND THE SUDEL FELD MOUNTAINS IN THE BACK. IN SUMMER, HIKING, CYCLING, PARAGLIDING. SWIMMING IN THE SCHLIERSEE, THIERSEE OR THE TEGERNSEE. IN WINTER ENDLESS KILOMETERS OF CROSS-COUNTRY TRAILS IN BAYRISCHZELL AND FISCHBACHAU, THE SKI RESORTS SUDELFELD AND PITZINGSEE. MUNICH'S CULTURE, SIGHTSEEING IN SALZBURG, THE KUFSTEIN ROUND THE CORNER. THE FELLOW VALUE PRODUCERS IN THE COUNTRY. AND ALWAYS: COMING BACK TO THE HOLIDAY HOME. LYING UNDER THE TREES AND READING. HAVING A LOOK ON THE FIRE IN THE CHIMNEY LOUNGE AND PLAYING THE FAVORITE SONG ON THE WURLITZER...

View of the hut tower at night.
Orangery.

INFORMATION. ARCHITECTS>
HK ARCHITEKTEN // 2007.
HUT> 500 SQM // 72 GUESTS //
11 BEDROOMS // 2 BATHROOMS.
ADDRESS> DORNAUBERG 110,
GINZLING, AUSTRIA.
WWW.OLPERERHUETTE.DE

Dining area with panoramic window.
Exterior view. Olpererhutte and mountains.
The complex surrounded by nature.

Olpererhütte

GINZLING, AUSTRIA

The Olpererhütte is situated in the Zillertal Nature Park at 2,389 meters above sea level, above Mount Schlegeis-speicher (1,782 meters). Guests can enjoy the sun all day long due to its south-facing location on Mount Riepenkar, just below the Olperer (3,467 meters), the third largest peak of the Zillertal Alps. Olpererhütte offers a great view across the lake to the main Zillertal alpine ridge, including the glacier field and the three peaks of Mount Gran Pilastro (Hochfeiler, 3,510 meters), Grande Mésule (Großer Moseler, 3,473 meters) and Punta Bianca (Hoher Weißzint, 3,371 meters). It is located on the long-distance hiking trail number 502 going from Munich to Venice, on the Zillertal trek, the Berlin High Trail as well as the Neumarkter Runde, a panoramic high-altitude trekking route existing since 2006. The house, built in 1881 by the Prague Section of the Olpererhütte, is one of the early shelters of the Eastern Alps. The aim at that time was to make the ascent of Mount Olperer more "comfortable". It was also intended to simplify tours to Mount Fußstein, the Gefrorene-Wand-Spitzen and the Schrammacher. After being purchased by the Berlin Section in 1900, the hut took on additional importance as a base on the Berlin High Trail. In 2004, the Berlin Section, sold the hut to the Neumarkt Section. The Olpererhütte was rebuilt by the Neumarkt Section in the years from 2005 to 2007. The opening took place in 2008, and today it gives the opportunity to have a relaxing time out in a house designed from natural materials, which radiates a warm and homely atmosphere inside and reveals wonderful views of the beautiful nature outside.

Exterior view. Surroundings.

Exterior view. Cabin with mountains.
View of the sunset.

GETTING AROUND. THE OFFER FOR ACTIVE AND PASSIVE RECREATION IN THE IMMEDIATE VICINITY OF THE OLPERERHÜTTE IS EXCELLENT. THE NEUMARKTER RUNDE TREK IS PARTICULARLY WORTH MENTIONING. WITHIN 4.5 HOURS OF WALKING, YOU WILL EXPERIENCE A BREATHTAKING AND DIVERSE NATURAL SPECTACLE. PASSING WATERFALLS AND A RESERVOIR YOU REACH THE OLPERERHÜTTE – ONLY A FEW METERS FURTHER YOU FIND THE STUNNING SUSPENSION BRIDGE, WHICH OFFERS AN INCREDIBLE VIEW OVER THE TURQUOISE BLUE SCHLEGEISS RESERVOIR.

INFORMATION. ARCHITECT>
ELMAR UNTERHAUSER EU ARCHITECTS
// 2017. HOLIDAY APARTMENTS>
582.50 SQM // 24 GUESTS //
9 BEDROOMS // 9 BATHROOMS.
ADDRESS> OTTO HUBER-STRASSE 19,
MERANO, ITALY.
WWW.DESIREEMERAN.COM

Interior view of a bedroom. Staircase.
Exterior view of the garden.

Désirée Design Apartments

MERANO, ITALY

The new apartment house and the associated 19th-century villa is situated in the middle of a quiet chestnut avenue near the old town of Merano. The new four-story apartment building is characterized by unusual construction dimensions and its dynamic shape. Each corner of the building has cantilevered elements that are part of the apartments and terraces that are delimited by glass balustrades. The design concept of breaking down what would usually be a uniform structure into different volumes that face each other at different levels, is based on several considerations. First, the twisted volumes of the building create several visual axes; then, it diminishes the building's physical presence making it look less tall.

The torsion of the volume visible at each level creates covered outdoor areas at all the apartments' corners, which can be used as terraces or balconies. All this is accompanied by a lighting that gives the building an elegant and exciting look in the evening. All apartments, consisting of a living room and kitchen area and a separate sleeping area, are exposed to light, and ventilated from three sides.

The main staircase and the elevator in the center of the building form a cylindrical hollow volume, the core of the new building. The rotation of the individual levels creates interesting, spatial outdoor areas, while the façade openings in different shapes and sizes give life to the white-plastered surface of the building.

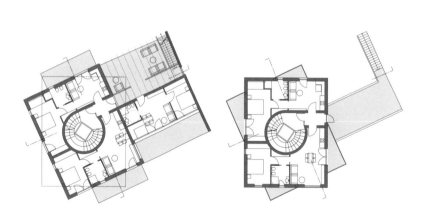

GETTING AROUND. A HUGE RANGE OF ACTIVITIES IS AVAILABLE: THERE ARE MANY SKI RESORTS SUCH AS MERANO 2000, SCHNALS VALLEY, ULTENTAL AND SCHWEMMALM ARE JUST AS ATTRACTIVE AS THE SPA TOWN OF MERANO WITH ITS SPA HOUSE, THE OLD TOWN THEATER, THE ART HOUSE AND THE TAPPEINER PROMENADE. THERE ARE COUNTLESS HIKING TRAILS TO BE EXPLORED ON THE SURROUNDING MOUNTAIN RANGES.

Exterior view with mountains. Floor plans.
The complex from garden.

Front view.
The complex by night.

INFORMATION. ARCHITECT>
LECHNER TOM – LP ARCHITEKTUR //
2016. HISTORIC FARMHOUSE>
200 SQM // 8–12 GUESTS //
4 BEDROOMS // 2 BATHROOMS.
ADDRESS> NEUBACH 2A,
ANNABERG-LUNGÖTZ,
SALZBURGERLAND, AUSTRIA.
WWW.KAETHUNDNANEI.AT

Vaulted cellar with wine stock. Detail doors.
Bathroom with sauna. A bedroom.
Exterior view from the garden.

Alpenchalet
Käth & Nanei

SALZBURGERLAND,
AUSTRIA

A very special house for very special people came back to life by preserving the old and bringing in the new, which unobtrusively provides comfort.

The Großschlaggut's history can be traced back to the 16th century. The farmhouse was renovated and the Käth & Nanei original and comfortable vacation home opened its doors in 2016 with the motto "Simply be ...". Restored according to 400-years-old construction methods, the house now offers space for up to 12 people. With four bedrooms, bathrooms, a country kitchen and the "Guten Stube", a ski and sports storage facility as well as a storage & creative space in the vaults. The rooms meet the high quality standards of a special vacation domicile. However, the possibility of renting an entire courtyard for yourself is rare.

The new historic Großschlaggut has this exclusivity, which offers every guest an authentic home for a few days or even weeks. This place can be booked for small events like weddings and anniversaries with catering by Max Pfeiffenberger of the Essgalerie company, for meetings to brainstorm and innovate, or there is the "Schmiedestätte" for meetings in a small circle. Relaxation areas such as the panoramic windows and the floating loungers in the orchard invite guests to regain energy and match the house's concept of creating a place that offers a superior sojourn quality.

Alpine chalet with snow.
Kitchen from the top.

View of the dining area. Interior view of bathroom. Floor plans.

GETTING AROUND. THE GROSSSCHLAGGUT FARM IN THE SALZBURGER LAMMERTAL VALLEY IN ANNABERG-LUNGÖTZ IS ALL ALONE ON A HIGH PLATEAU AT 950 M ABOVE SEA LEVEL. EXTENSIVE MEADOWS AND FORESTS SURROUND THE FARM AND THE MOUNTAIN RIDGES OF THE BISCHOFSMÜTZE AND DACHSTEIN MOUNTAINS LOOM MAJESTICALLY BEHIND THE FARMHOUSE.

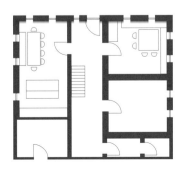

INFORMATION. CONCEPT> SEBASTIAN HATZFELDT // 2015. CHALET> 110 SQM // 4–6 GUESTS // 2 BEDROOMS // 2 BATHROOMS. ADDRESS> MOOSALPSTRASSE 247, TÖRBEL, SWITZERLAND. WWW.CHALET-AVANTGARDE.CH

Exterior chalet. Interior view of the kitchen and living room. A bedroom.

Chalet Avantgarde

TÖRBEL, SWITZERLAND

The Chalet Avantgarde is different from the common look of "heavy beams", regarding its roof construction, and thus this way the locally prescribed chalet exterior style meets the present. It follows the concept of visual lightness. The chalet was built combining high-class design and construction details with excellent craftsmanship.

The use of plywood with extra inlays instead of heavy beams made it possible to build a very filigree-looking roof overhang. This contrasts sharply with the usual roofs in the alpine region. The interior is characterized by both exclusive and explicitly modern-looking knotless larch wood of Swiss origin, which probably has never been realized in this consistent way in an alpine chalet. The symbiosis of calmness on the one hand and adequate diversity of the

wood pattern on the other hand is what is so convincing. The warm tone of the larch wood is optimally accentuated by a final oil treatment. For entertainment, the cottage offers a 78-inch home cinema, an excellent music system and a library with a great selection of books.

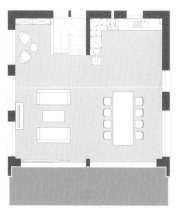

GETTING AROUND. NESTLED IN A UNIQUE LANDSCAPE, THE VIEW OPENS DIRECTLY ONTO NINE 4,000-METER PEAKS OF NO LESS THAN THREE MOUNTAIN MASSIFS, AND 1,000 METERS DOWN INTO THE ZERMATT VALLEY. IN SUMMER THERE IS THE GROSSE ALP WITH 130 COWS, AND FROM MID-OCTOBER THE LARCHES BECOME A GOLDEN SEA OF COLORS. IN WINTER THERE ARE LOTS OF HIKING TRAILS AND THE SKIING AREA MOOSALP, WHICH IS ONLY ONE KILOMETER AWAY. THE MAJOR SKIING AREAS OF ZERMATT, SAAS FEE AND GRÄCHEN ARE EASILY ACCESSIBLE.

Chalet in the snow. Floor plans.
Front view.

Living room with panoramic windows. Detail of the
reading area. Bottom view of the house.

INFORMATION. ARCHITECTS>
FEUERSINGER ARCHITEKTUR // 2020.
APARTMENTS> 90 AND 120 SQM //
4–6 GUESTS AND 6–9 GUESTS //
2 AND 3 BEDROOMS //
2 BATHROOMS EACH APARTMENT.
ADDRESS> POSTPLATTENSTRASSE 20,
HOF BEI SALZBURG, AUSTRIA.
WWW.HAUSUNDHOF-SALZBURG.AT

haus und hof

HOF BEI SALZBURG, AUSTRIA

The three quiet and tastefully designed apartments, built into the slope, surprisingly appear modest at first sight. The building is characterized by minimalism and reduction. There are as little different shapes as possible. As few different materials as possible. As much warmth as possible. One thing that really sticks out is the black color.

The black timber façade fits perfectly with the green nature respectively in winter with the white snowy landscape. The interior walls also have the black color. This matches perfectly with the concrete floor and the wooden walls. The highlight of the apartments are the atria, providing not only pleasant light, but also exude an extraordinary calm.

The interior of the apartments is characterized by custom-made furniture and designer objects, and they differ in character due to the small details that have been added with care and individual color schemes. The "down-to-earth apartment" reflects earthiness and closeness to nature, the "active apartment" stands for sportiness, freshness and the "design-loving apartment" for design at the highest level.

View of the living area with atrium.
Kitchen and dining area. Large windows.
Exterior view from the garden.

Interior view of an apartment. Wooden bench detail.
Bathroom. Floor plan.

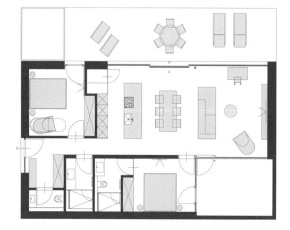

GETTING AROUND. THE HAUS UND HOF IS LOCATED RIGHT BETWEEN THE SALZKAMMERGUT AND THE CITY OF SALZBURG AND IS SURROUNDED BY LAKES AND MOUNTAINS. LAKES FUSCHLSEE, ATTERSEE, MONDSEE, WOLFGANGSEE, HINTERSEE AND THE WONDERFUL MOUNTAINS LIKE THE SCHOBER AND SCHAFBERG, THE ZWÖLFERHORN AND THE ALMKOGEL CAN BE SEEN STRAIGHT FROM THE TERRACES OF THE APARTMENTS. MORE THAN FIVE GOLF COURSES ARE NEARBY AND OFFER ALTERNATIVE OUTDOOR ACTIVITIES. THE CITY OF SALZBURG IS VERY CLOSE AND OFFERS CULTURAL AND URBAN DIVERSION.

Exterior view.
Top-down view of the atrium.

INFORMATION. ARCHITECT>
IKE IKRATH // 2014. 5 LOFTS>
100–120 SQM // 2–12 GUESTS.
ADDRESS> TOSCANINIWEG 10,
BAD GASTEIN, AUSTRIA.
WWW.ALPENLOFTS.COM

*Bedroom with panoramic window. View from the
balcony. Kitchen and living area.*

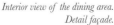

Interior view of the dining area.
Detail façade.

Alpenlofts

BAD GASTEIN, AUSTRIA

Owned and designed by Ike Ikrath, a renowned architect, and his creative network, the Alpenlofts are known for their forward-thinking and low-impact designs. As a set of five tucked-away and hidden lofts, the holiday homes are nestled among the alpine hills of Bad Gastein, a progressive, edgy village in the Austrian Alps. Unique and individual, each space acts as a conversation between the interior and exterior world, between the power and the nurture of the mountains.

Built with floor-to-ceiling windows overlooking the valley, the lodges each feature a private sauna, fireplace, all year covered porch, and designer furniture from Charles and Ray Eames, Josef Frank, Hans J Wegner – plus amenities by Iittala, Löwe, Laufen, and Miele. Full of intention from start to finish,

all the materials used were either sourced from the region or made by local craftsmen. The open construction floor plan highlights the visible timber beams, natural stones, and solid woods used as part of a holistic, creative, and low-impact solution for conscious alpine luxury.

Camillo – Minimalist and contemporary, co-designed by Elma Choung as an homage to traditional alpine interiors.
Tessa – Refined and elevated with muted colors, a centerpiece fireplace, and super-panoramic windows.
Rosa – Casual and intimate with wishbone chairs by Hans J Wegner.
Ed – Distinguished and masculine with retro leather and deep, dark oak floors.
Madero – A bohemian chalet for art lovers, color enthusiasts and quirky hearts.

Terrace with mountain view.
Living area.

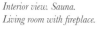
Interior view. Sauna.
Living room with fireplace.

GETTING AROUND. BAD GASTEIN
IS A SMALL, ALPINE VILLAGE NESTLED
AMONG THE HIGH AUSTRIAN ALPS.
KNOWN FOR ITS HEALING THERMAL
WATERS, UNIQUE CITYSCAPE,
AWARD-WINNING ART FESTIVAL,
AND HISTORIC CITY CENTER
FEATURING BELLE EPOQUE AND
BRUTALIST ARCHITECTURE, THE
VILLAGE BOASTS A GIANT WATERFALL
IN THE MIDDLE OF TOWN. THE
ALPENLOFTS ARE LOCATED RIGHT
AT THE FOOTHILLS OF MOUNT
GRAUKOGEL (2,492 M) A 10-MINUTE
WALK FROM ITS CHAIRLIFT –
OFFERING GREAT SUMMER &
WINTER ACTIVITIES SUCH AS TRAIL
RUNNING, HIKING, MOUNTAIN LAKES
AND HUTS, SKIING AND SKI TOURS.

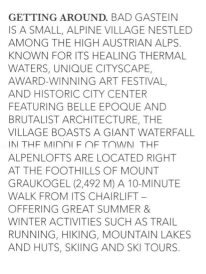

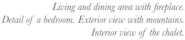
Living and dining area with fireplace.
Detail of a bedroom. Exterior view with mountains.
Interior view of the chalet.

Sporer Alm Chalet Geigerin

ZILLERTAL, TYROL,
AUSTRIA

The small, exclusive chalet village is located high up at 1,200 meters above sea level on the Rohrberg, in the heart of the beautiful Zillertal. The Sporer Alm consists of four detached luxury chalets, which are in harmony with the surrounding alpine landscape. The idyllic chalets are built almost exclusively from recycled wood and have a surface of 130 and to 190 square meters. The planks and beams got their unique look through the influence of decades of wind, rain, sun as well as the use by human hands. The houses convey a lot of warmth, space, security and tranquility for their guests and promise a wonderful stay. In 2020, the retreat was upgraded with a few additional amenities. A natural pool, carports and a special room used for enjoyment as well as a further, cozy chalet complete the Sporer Alm. Geigerin, the new, private chalet offers 140 square meters of space for two to four people and plenty of free room on the 1,200-square-meter property. The interior design consists of an balanced interplay of wood, fine fabrics, as well as of natural materials and elements from the past, which have been lovingly refurbished and put in a new light. The high-class chalets' large living and dining area with tiled stove and a reading corner as well as a fully equipped kitchen with a wine cabinet with climate control and a cozy bar are on the ground floor. The private garden with a south-facing terrace is the perfect place to relax in the sauna and whirlpool. The gallery, two bedrooms and two bathrooms en suite are located on the first floor. The balcony offers a wonderful panoramic view across the valley.

INFORMATION. ARCHITECTS>
GA-DESIGN GMBH // INTERIOR
DESIGN > LEO WOHNARCHITEKTUR //
2020. CHALET> 140 SQM // 4 GUESTS
// 2 BEDROOMS // 3 BATHROOMS.
ADDRESS> ROHRBERG 107, ZILLERTAL,
TYROL, AUSTRIA.
WWW.SPORER-ALM.COM

GETTING AROUND. ZILLERTAL ARENA SKI AND HIKING AREA, FICHTENSCHLOSS CASTLE, FICHTENSEE LAKE, SUMMER TOBOGGAN RUN ARENA COASTER, E-BIKE RENTAL, THE ZELL AM ZILLER RECREATIONAL PARK INCLUDING A TENNIS COURT, AN ICE RINK, A PLAYGROUND, A SOCCERFIELD, A MINIGOLF COURSE, A SWIMMING POOL AND A VOLLEYBALL COURT, THE ZILLERTAL RAILROAD WITH THE STEAM LOCOMOTIVE, A FARM EXHIBITION AND ALPINE DAIRY, THE KRIMML WATERFALLS, THE MARIA RAST CROSSROADS IN HAINZENBERG, A GOLD MINE WITH A GOLD PANNING CAMP AND A SMALL ANIMAL PARK IN HAINZENBERG, AN ALPACA HIKE THROUGH THE FOREST IN THE VILLAGE OF STUMM.

A bedroom. Interior view of the living room. Kitchen detail.

Kitchen with dining area. Detail furniture. Bathroom and bedroom.

INFORMATION. ARCHITECTS>
BERGMEISTERWOLF // 2020.
HOTEL> 1,050 SQM // 24 GUESTS //
12 BEDROOMS // 12 BATHROOMS.
ADDRESS> DORFSTRASSE 73,
VAHRN, ITALY.
WWW.VILLAMAYR.COM

View of the common area. Interior view.
Exterior view of the Villa Mayr.

Villa Mayr

VAHRN, ITALY

Villa Mayr tells the story of a house with an eventful past, a promising present as well as a promising future. Villa Mayr reflects a return to the origins and, at the same time, a process of continued development. It stands for building on tradition and enhancing details that transform the house into a lovingly and carefully designed boutique hotel. On the first floor, by removing a wall, a space continuum of bar, foyer and reception is born, which looks as if it is growing into the interior. The historic components such as the staircase and the parlor were sensitively refurbished and staged.

A play of color and materiality creates a warm atmosphere and infuses the well-designed rooms with a high-quality, home-like character. The architects bergmeisterwolf have responded with great bravura to finding a balance between existing and new structures. The extension of existing structures, working with projections and recesses, dealing with the historical substance and the integration of the wooden façade make Villa Mayr a house with a signature, where guests enjoy staying.

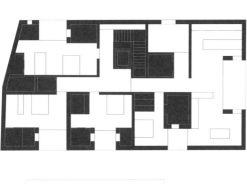

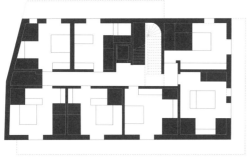

GETTING AROUND. THE LANDSCAPE OF VARNA (VAHRN), A SUBURB OF THE CITY OF BRESSANONE, ONLY A FEW KILOMETERS AWAY, IS CHARACTERIZED BY VINEYARDS, BLOSSOMING APPLE ORCHARDS AND CHESTNUT GROVES. THE RANGE OF LEISURE ACTIVITIES IS LARGE AND VARIED, IN SUMMER AND WINTER. THERE IS A GREAT OFFER OF ACTIVITIES FOR WALKERS AND CYCLISTS IN THE MOUNTAINS AND VALLEYS, AND THE PLOSE SKI AREA IS ONLY 20 MINUTES AWAY. BRESSANONE ITSELF IS AN ATTRACTION WITH ITS OLD TOWN AND THE PICTURESQUE ARCADES, THE CATHEDRAL AND MANY CULTURAL OFFERS.

Main view from the garden. Floor plans.
Panoramic view from the long balcony.

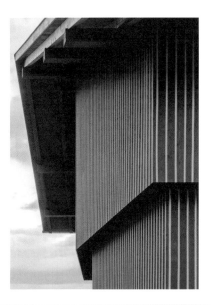

View of the common dining area. Façade detail.
View of the common leisure area.

INFORMATION. ARCHITECTS>
LAKONIS ARCHITEKTEN // 2014.
HOUSE> 310 SQM // 5–8 GUESTS //
7 BEDROOMS // 4 BATHROOMS.
ADDRESS> SEESTRASSE 31,
TRAUNKIRCHEN, AUSTRIA.
WWW.TRAUNSEE31.AT

Terrace with panoramic view. See 31 with snow.
Dining area. Living area with panoramic windows.

SEE 31

TRAUNKIRCHEN,
AUSTRIA

State-of-the-art architecture between mountains and water. In summer 2014, a unique new vacation destination was born in the Salzkammergut region. Two wooden houses directly on Lake Traunsee, surrounded by generous flower meadows, trees and mountains. The layout of the two wooden houses refers to the characteristic scattered settlements of the region.

With 150 square meters, one house offers space for six to eight people, the second cube includes two 80-square-meter apartments, each of which can accommodate up to five people. Each house's center is a spacious combined cooking and living area. Contemporary comfort and the selection of only a few, preferably untreated materials as well as an unrestricted view over the lake to the Traunstein were the essential parameters of the design. Precious surfaces made of regional materials – oiled solid larch wood, felt, stone, glass – and high-quality interior and exterior design give the interior its unique atmosphere. The compact bedrooms, together with the apartment's own sauna as well as the fireplace, constitute a perfect place of rest. All the complex is located on an idyllic beach.

The house from the lake.
Bathroom with sauna.

*Living area with fireplace. Sleeping area
with panoramic view. Exterior view in winter.
Floor plans.*

GETTING AROUND. TRAUNKIRCHEN IS A PICTURESQUE RESORT IN THE SALZKAMMERGUT REGION, WHICH IS CHARACTERIZED BY THE IMPRESSIVE BACKDROP OF THE TRAUNSTEIN MOUNTAIN. NOT ONLY CULTURE AND LANDSCAPE ARE WORTH A TRIP, YOU CAN ALSO EXPLORE THE MYSTICAL WORLD OF THE DRIPSTONE CAVES. THERE IS ALSO A LOT OF WINTER SPORTS TO DO. THE SKIING AREA OF THE FEUERKOGEL AS WELL AS THE DACHSTEIN MOUNTAINS ARE WITHIN EASY REACH. THE TRAUNSEE LAKE ITSELF OFFERS A WIDE RANGE OF ACTIVITIES FOR WATER SPORTS AND BATHING AFICIONADOS. THE GLÖCKLERLAUF IS A GREAT EVENT OF MANY TRADITIONAL EVENTS OF TRAUNKIRCHEN.

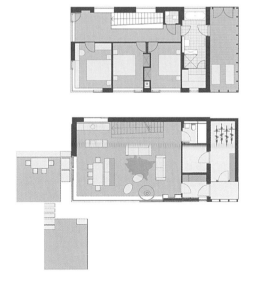

General view of the village.
Eat-in kitchen. View from the garden.
Bedroom.

Hüs üf der Flüe

ERNEN, SWITZERLAND

The Hüs üf der Flüe 6 was built between 1424 and 1454 and is one of the oldest and best preserved traditional "Heidenhaus" (house of the heathens) in Goms. This house in the typical valaisan style was carefully renovated in 2016 and offers a splendid view over the whole valley.

This architectural monument has two 3.5-room apartments, which can be rented individually or all together. Each apartment has its own garden. Both apartments have a large kitchen, a living room, two bedrooms and a bathroom. The ground floor apartment is equipped with an old stone stove from 1576 and with an antique buffet from 1822 in the living room. The upper apartment has its own entrance on the first floor, where a new staircase connects to the first floor. In the kitchen there is the typical

wooden chimney of the old Goms houses and even its original cross has been preserved.

The house was renovated with much love and respect for its history. The hosts attached great importance selecting the materials to be used in the house. Thus, the kitchens and the dining tables, as well as the large beds, are made of old wood, left over from the renovation. Historical building lovers and people looking for an authentic atmosphere will feel at home in the Hüs üf der Flüe. In winter the house is comfortably warm thanks to the district heating system. People wishing to have a little more of cozy atmosphere can also light the fire in the stone stove.

INFORMATION. ARCHITECTS>
ABGOTTSPON WERLEN ARCHITEKTEN
// 2016. HISTORIC "HEATHEN HOUSE">
2 APARTMENTS, 85 SQM EACH // 4
GUESTS EACH // 2 BEDROOMS EACH //
1 BATHROOM EACH. ADDRESS>
FLÜE 11, ERNEN, SWITZERLAND.
WWW.MUNTS-PAVLICEK.CH

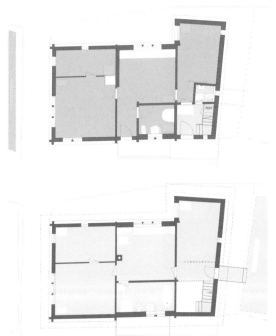

GETTING AROUND. ERNEN IS ONE OF THE MOST BEAUTIFUL VILLAGES IN SWITZERLAND. THE SMALL VILLAGE IN THE UPPER VALAIS, SITUATED ON A SUNNY SLOPE AT 1,200 M ABOVE SEA LEVEL, HAS A UNIQUE AND CHARMING CULTURAL LANDSCAPE. ERNEN IS ALSO KNOWN FOR ITS MUSIC SCENE. HIKING, BIKING, ENJOYING THE SILENCE: ALL THIS IS POSSIBLE IN THE BINNTAL LANDSCAPE PARK NEXT DOOR. THE REGIONAL NATURE PARK OFFERS AN AMAZING VARIETY OF TREASURES. IN WINTER THE ALETSCHARENA SKIING AREA IS EASILY ACCESSIBLE BY BUS.

Bedroom. Floor plan.
Free-standing bathtub.

Kitchen-living room and living room.
Detail of an old chest.
Exterior view of the shingle façade.

INFORMATION. ARCHITECTS>
NATURBAU GSCHWEND // 2021.
CHALET> 15,000 SQM // 30 GUESTS //
1–2 BEDROOMS PER CHALET //
1–2 BATHROOMS PER CHALET.
ADDRESS> BACH 69, BACH, AUSTRIA.
WWW.BENGLERWALD.AT

Benglerwald Berg Chaletdorf

BACH, AUSTRIA

Overlooking the Lech River, at an altitude of 1,200 meters, surrounded by mountains and peaks, blessed with a great view, the sunny Benglerwald plateau is considered one of the most beautiful places in the Lech Valley. This unique landscape nestles the Benglerwald alpine chalet village. It consists of some hideaways that turn a mountain break into a time of private luxury. The crystalline alpine lake is a refreshing natural bathing spot in the sun. There are a total of 15,000 square meters of space to unwind and relax Benglerwald mountain chalet village. Its nine luxury chalets in the mountains with five-star service what Benglerwald Berg Chaletdorf offers to its guests. Chalets with gym, a chalet for romantic getaways, a fully fenced dog chalet, a family chalet and other highly comfortable refuges are available in the breathtaking mountains of the Lech Valley. Each chalet includes a spa deluxe with hot tub and sauna, some have a wellness tub and shower and are equipped with gym and yoga equipment. Gourmets feel like they're in heaven when the Genussmanufaktur invites to a culinary event with alpine specialties or shows off its selection of Dry Aged Beef. The exclusivity of the chalets in the middle of nature is evident: the kitchens are fully equipped, they have an open fireplace and an effect fire, a smart home equipment and free WLAN.

Chalet from the garden. A bedroom. Kitchen. Exterior with panoramic view.

Chalet in the snow. Jacuzzi from the top.
Bedroom detail. Layout map.

GETTING AROUND. THE LECHTAL IS MOST ENCHANTING BECAUSE OF ITS BEAUTY AND SCENIC DIVERSITY. IT EXTENDS TO THE BORDER OF THE VORARLBERG REGION AND THE FAMOUS SKIING AREA OF WARTH/SCHRÖCKEN AT THE ARLBERG. IN SUMMER AS WELL AS IN WINTER, THE LECHTAL OFFERS A WIDE RANGE OF ACTIVITIES: IN WINTER, THE SKIING AREA "JÖCHELSPITZE" OFFERS GREAT SKIING OPPORTUNITIES. IN SUMMER, THE LECHTAL VALLEY IS HOME TO A NUMBER OF BEAUTIFUL HIKING AND BIKING TRAILS, FOR EXAMPLE THE BEAUTIFUL LANDSCAPE ALONG THE EUROPEAN LONG-DISTANCE TRAIL, THE LECHWEG, WHICH RUNS THROUGH THE LECHTAL NATURE PARK REGION.

Benglerwald mountain chalet village.
Bathtub with panoramic view.

INFORMATION. ARCHITECTS>
OFIS ARCHITECTS // 2021.
HOTEL> 5,800 SQM // 138 GUESTS //
69 BEDROOMS // 69 BATHROOMS.
ADDRESS> RIBČEV LAZ 45, BOHINJSKO
JEZERO, SLOWENIA.
WWW.HOTELBOHINJ.SI

*Interior view common room. View of the
dining area. Exterior view with mountains.*

Hotel Bohinj

BOHINJSKO JEZERO,
SLOVENIA

Hotel Bohinj, renovated in recent years, is located on a plateau in the middle of the Triglav National Park. The new owners modified the structure of the building and the interior design, paying attention to sustainable standards and local architectural tradition. Existing building material was recycled, local larch wood and only a little concrete were used, and a modern, energy-efficient utility system was installed. A wooden structure wraps the existing building and protects it from earthquakes. The lobby and restaurant are located in an annex that has a roofed entrance. Triangular elements with ornaments reflect the old gable roofs and mountain peaks. The hotel has 69 rooms of various sizes with panoramic windows and balconies, a two-story entrance hall, a restaurant, a retro bistro with a traditional

terracotta oven, a small meeting room and a club with a wine shop. In terms of structure, the corridors are reminiscent of typical Bohinj barns. Patterns and materials, wall coverings and furniture made of local larch wood, as well as ceilings discreetly pick up folk style elements that threaten to disappear.

Much of the interior furnishings were designed especially for the hotel, such as chairs made from recycled plastic bottles. The floors of the common areas are in light gray echoing the color of the surrounding rocks, while the pathway to the entrance is made of black Slovenian stone, making it eye-catching. The hotel has a spa area with a heated outdoor pool; a room with a large fireplace is available for events. The facility is barely illuminated; in this way, guests can enjoy the night sky to the fullest.

GETTING AROUND. NEARBY BOHINJ LAKE IS ONE OF THE CLEANEST LAKES OF THE COUNTRY AND A GREAT PLACE TO GO FOR A SWIM. MOUNTAINS AND THE CHURCH OF JANEZ KRSTNIK ARE ALSO VERY CLOSE, AS WELL AS SMALL, IDYLLIC VILLAGES WITH THEIR TRADITIONAL BOHINJ BARNS. FLOWER LOVERS CAN VISIT THE BOTANICAL GARDENS SITUATED ALL OVER THE VALLEYS AND MOUNTAINS OF THE REGION.

Hotel Bohinj from outside.
Floor plan. Interior view.

Balcony with panoramic view.
Detail bathroom. Interior view of a bedroom.

INFORMATION. ARCHITECTS>
BIRGIT DOSSER (CHALET), HANNES
NIEDERSTÄTTER (CONSTRUCTION LAW
CONSULTING CHALET), MANUEL
BENEDIKTER (NATURRESIDENCE),
BIRGIT DOSSER (INTERIOR DESIGN
AND GARDEN NATURRESIDENCE)
// 2010 NATURRESIDENCE AND 2014
CHALET. APARTMENTS AND CHALET>
40–60 SQM AND 95 SQM // 12 AND 4
GUESTS // 5 VACATION APARTMENTS
AND TWO UNITS IN THE CHALET.
ADDRESS> PICHLERSTRASSE 26,
SCHENNA, SOUTH TYROL, ITALY.
WWW.DAHOAM.IT

*Naturresidence with swimming pool. Exterior view
chalet. Chalet living area.*

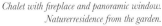

Chalet with fireplace and panoramic window.
Naturerresidence from the garden.

Dahoam Naturresidence and Dahoam Chalet

SOUTH TYROL, ITALY

Two things immediately catch the eye when you arrive at Naturresidence Dahoam: the extraordinary view of the Merano valley and the modern architecture of the building. The house is situated on a beautiful slope above the village of Schenna and faces southwest. This not only brings a lot of sunlight to the spacious balconies and thus delights the guests, it is also an important part of the sustainable, energetic and ecological concept that was implemented using passive building methods. In addition to the active and passive use of solar energy and the use of regional woods, rainwater is also collected and used.

There are five apartments available. The lodging's furnishing is modern and there are large window openings providing views of the surrounding mountain peaks and giving access to the garden with its natural swimming pond and an outdoor Finnish sauna. The Dahoam Chalet is not far away and likewise situated in a sunny panoramic location.

The building, made of untreated local larch, is a modern interpretation of the typical local barn. It was built in energy-efficient and sustainable construction on the basement of a house from the 60s. Each of the two floors is a 95-square-meter chalet with 54 square meters of living space and a terrace of 41 square meters. The apartments are characterized by the panoramic view of Merano, the natural materials, as well as a harmonious color concept. They are equipped with a wood-burning stove and a Finnish sauna, what makes them a real feel-good oasis with space for two people each.

Chalet surrounded by the Merano valley.
Bedroom Naturresidence. View in winter.
Living room Naturresidence. Floor plans.

GETTING AROUND. WALKS ON THE WHALE PATH, HIGH ALTITUDE HIKES IN SCHENNA'S POPULAR HIKING AREAS, CYCLING TOURS, WINTER BREAKS. THE NORTHERNMOST PROVINCE OF ITALY IMPRESSES WITH MANY ATTRACTIONS: ITS INNOVATIVE ARCHITECTURE IN DIALOGUE WITH TRADITIONS AND LANDSCAPE, ITS DIVERSE NATURE, FROM ALPINE MOUNTAIN RANGES TO MEDITERRANEAN WINE LANDSCAPES, AND ITS CUISINE INFLUENCED BY AUSTRIA AND ITALY MAKE THE REGION A PERFECT DESTINATION FOR ARCHITECTURE LOVERS, HIKERS AND GOURMETS.

INFORMATION. ARCHITECTS> NOA*
NETWORK OF ARCHITECTURE // 2018.
HOTEL> 2,000 SQM // 50 GUESTS //
25 BEDROOMS // 25 BATHROOMS.
ADDRESS> DORF 15, OBERBOZEN,
RITTEN, ITALY.
WWW.GLORIETTE-GUESTHOUSE.COM

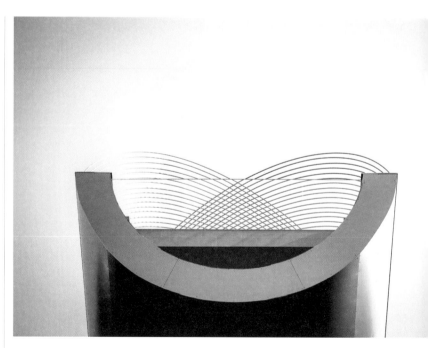

Exterior view. Interior view of the rooftop spa.
Infinity pool from below.

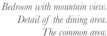

Bedroom with mountain view.
Detail of the dining area.
The common area.

Gloriette Guesthouse

RITTEN, ITALY

The Gloriette Guesthouse carries on the tradition of the Reno (Ritten) region summer resort and is a place where life is truly celebrated in style. It is not only cosmopolitans, gourmets and mountain lovers who find themselves at home in this relaxed atmosphere. Inspired by the timeless-elegant Art Nouveau architectural typology, tradition meets modern. The house with a heart and a nostalgic vibe raised in summer 2019. Everything that is hidden behind the façade with round arches can easily be read from the outside in an unmistakable way. Its greatest highlight is certainly the rooftop spa in the hipped roof. This is where the sauna and steam bath with floor-to-ceiling panoramic windows, expansive relaxation areas as well as a few intimate terraces are located and offer a pleasant stay in the fresh air. However, the Infinity Relax Pool is the absolute eye-catcher – a bronze-colored cylinder that cuts the south side of the hipped roof. The arch is turned upside down and led into the interior of the roof. Inside, you enter the center of the cylinder-shaped pool. A sliding door opens allowing to descend into the waters, floating in the well-tempered water towards the horizon.

From this point the owners' aesthetic aspirations for their charming guesthouse are consistent throughout the entire house. It is much more than just the first-class comfort that makes the 25 suites, but also the lounge bar and the Ristorantino so special. It is the little details, customized accessories and a touch of luxury that promise true relaxation.

Main view of the Gloriette Guesthouse.
Panoramic view from the infinity pool.

Interior view of a room. Sauna with floor-to-ceiling panoramic windows. Dining area. West view.

GETTING AROUND. A DIFFERENT RHYTHM AND PERCEPTION OF TIME AND NATURE PREVAILS AT THE MUNICIPALITY OF RENON (RITTEN). THE UNSPOILED LANDSCAPE OF THE MONS RITANUS OFFERS SEVERAL HIKING TRAILS, MTB ROUTES AND MANY PLACES TO GO. THE 360-DEGREE PANORAMA IS PARTICULARLY FASCINATING, STRETCHING FROM THE FABULOUS BACKDROP OF THE DOLOMITES TO BOLZANO AND THE PICTURESQUE VINEYARDS TO THE MIGHTY ORTLER MASSIF. BUT IF YOU ARE LOOKING FOR A LITTLE CHANGE AND WOULD LIKE TO TAKE A SHORT BREAK FROM THE BREAK, THE CABLE CAR WILL TAKE YOU RIGHT TO THE HEART OF BOLZANO'S CHARMING CITY LIFE IN JUST 12 MINUTES, WHERE YOU CAN ENJOY SHOPPING AND AN APERITIVO.

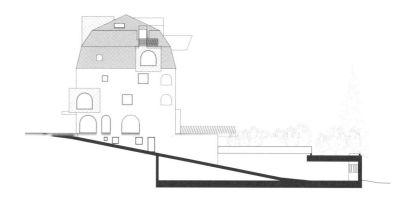

INFORMATION. ARCHITECT>
JÜRGEN HAGSPIEL // HUS9 2011 AND
LOFT7 2016. APARTMENTS> 58 AND
172 SQM // 10 GUESTS // 5 BEDROOMS
// 4 BATHROOMS. ADDRESS>
JÖRIHALDE 9, MITTELBERG,
KLEINWALSERTAL, AUSTRIA.
WWW.ALPEN-RAUM.AT

Interior view. Detail of a bedroom.
Main view.

Alpen-Raum Loft7 and Hus9

MITTELBERG, KLEINWALSERTAL,
AUSTRIA

When the conversion and general refurbishment of Loft7 and the new building at Hus9 were carried out, the aim was to achieve a high level of quality in harmony with nature. Both projects were mainly focused on simplicity, the reduction to the essentials and the renunciation of superfluous alpine kitsch.

It is modern yet down-to-earth and is built with local woods and honest materials from the region that are free of harmful additives such as varnishes, plasticizers, and colorants. Thanks to eco-friendly deep drilling, hot water generation by photovoltaics, wood from the own forest for cozy hours in front of the fireplace, a sustainable project that contributes to climate protection and a great eco-balance was implemented. Indoors, natural materials, warm colors

and well-planned details create a homely atmosphere and invite you to linger. Guests get family-like care and the hosts are happy to provide advice on excursion destinations, mountain tours, bad weather programs, help with guides, the ski school, mountaineering school and much more.

GETTING AROUND. THERE IS REALLY ONLY ONE WAY TO REACH KLEINWALSERTAL – VIA THE WALSERSCHANZ, A FORMER BORDERLINE BETWEEN GERMANY AND AUSTRIA. AT THE SAME TIME, NO OTHER AUSTRIAN HIGH MOUNTAIN VALLEY IS SO EASILY ACCESSIBLE FROM GERMANY. NO MATTER WHAT TIME OF THE YEAR – IT IS WORTH TO EXPLORE THE REGION – OUT AND ABOUT SKIING. IN SUMMER IT IS ALL ABOUT HIKING CROSSING BORDERS BETWEEN GERMANY AND AUSTRIA. IT IS THEN THAT NATURAL MARVELS LIKE THE GOTTESACKER PLATEAU, THE NATURAL BRIDGE OR THE BREITACHKLAMM GORGE SHOW THEIR BEAUTY IN ALL THEIR GLORY.

*View from the garden. Kitchen with dining area.
Sleeping area.*

*Detail of a bedroom. Interior view
kitchen. Exterior view.*

INFORMATION. ARCHITECTS>
ARCHITEKTEN GEMEINSCHAFT 4 AG,
AARAU AND LUZERN // 2015.
GUESTHOUSE> 371 SQM // 15 GUESTS
// 7 BEDROOMS // 7 BATHROOMS.
ADDRESS> MATHON, GRISONS,
SWITZERLAND.
WWW.LARESCH.CH

*The common dining area. View of one of the
bedrooms. Front view from the garden.*

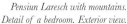

Pensiun Laresch with mountains.
Detail of a bedroom. Exterior view.

Pensiun Laresch

MATHON, SWITZERLAND

The village of Mathon in the middle of the Beverin Nature Park is characterized by a wild and unique landscape. This location demands very special architecture. The call for dealing carefully with the surroundings was joined by the task of developing a functional house with high design standards.

A "guesthouse", which should be a "house for guests" in every detail. The interior is dominated by natural and warm materials such as wood and clay, which provide a cozy atmosphere. The building is oriented in a way that guarantees fantastic views of the Alps from every room. The front window openings are set in a strict geometric way, while the different and distinctive framing creates a modern and well-proportioned façade image that plays with the soft lines of the surroundings. The half-meter masonry does not need any additional insulation and, together with the regional, precisely used materials, it makes the building sustainable and creates a pleasant indoor climate. Pensiun Laresch has seven rooms and a tiny house. It is also thanks to the warmth of the hosts that this wonderful place to recharge and relish has come to life.

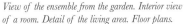
*View of the ensemble from the garden. Interior view
of a room. Detail of the living area. Floor plans.*

GETTING AROUND. DURING
WINTER, YOU CAN ENJOY GLITTERING
SNOW CRYSTALS, SUNSHINE AND
A CLOUDLESS SKY. IF YOU WANT
TO BE ACTIVE, YOU WILL FIND A LOT
OF DIVERSE SKI RUNS AND SLIDE
PATHS AT THE PIZ BEVERIN MOUNTAIN
AND IN THE SURROUNDINGS. PART
OF THEM IS ILLUMINATED AT NIGHT.
IN THE ROMANTIC FOREST GLAZE AT
THE SLEDDING TRAIL DROS MATHON/
LOHN YOU WILL FIND THE TIPI TENT,
WHERE DRINKS AND GRILLED
SPECIALTIES ARE SERVED. HIKING,
CLIMBING GARDEN, AND CULTURAL
TRIPS ARE AVAILABLE ALL YEAR.
FOR RELAXATION AND WELLNESS,
THE SPA OF ANDEER IS AT YOUR
DISPOSAL.

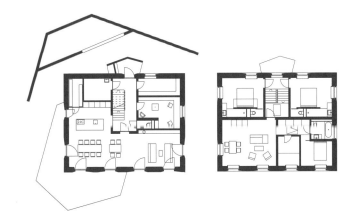

INFORMATION. ARCHITECTS>
BERGMEISTERWOLF AND
ARMIN SADER // 2017. CHALET>
280 SQM // 13 GUESTS //
6 BEDROOMS // 6 BATHROOMS.
ADDRESS> PALMSCHOSS 292,
BRESSANONE, ITALY.
WWW.ODLES-LODGE.COM

Interior view suite.
Room with terrace.

Exterior view of Odles Lodge.
Interior view. Detail of the green roof.

Odles Lodge

BRESSANONE, ITALY

These four suites connecting with the base of the building (garage), rotate around a common courtyard. The house thereby merges with the local conditions and becomes one with the landscape and the site. Following the pattern of the houses in the neighborhood, traditional materials such as wood and stone were used: natural stone for the plinth zone and quartered tree trunks for the façade. The house built on the hillside is designed following the topography and it is breaking where it encounters the terrain's edge. It's about the building rising out of and growing together with the landscape, a rotation.

The building's positioning creates a special courtyard situation in the rear area, a view towards the glade, a quiet place within nature. The wooden upper part is supported by a stone base and follows the height and shape of the surrounding roofscape. The openings in the façade are well placed to create open vistas and provide panoramic views of the landscape. The result is a dynamic flow that incorporates the surroundings without restricting the neighbors' perceptions and views.

Bedroom with panoramic window. Terrace.

Built-in furniture and fireplace. Sauna.
View of Odles Lodge.

GETTING AROUND. THE ODLES LODGE IS LOCATED AT AN ALTITUDE OF ALMOST 2,000 M ON MOUNT PLOSE, ONLY 30 MINUTES FROM BRESSANONE VIS À VIS OF THE DOLOMITES, THE UNESCO WORLD NATURAL HERITAGE. THE CLIMATE, AIR AND THE PUREST WATER OF THE PLOSE GUARANTEE A RELAXING STAY. AT ODLES LODGE THE ADVENTURE FOR HIKERS, MOUNTAIN CLIMBERS, MOUNTAIN BIKERS AND SKIERS BEGINS RIGHT IN FRONT OF THE DOOR.

INFORMATION. ARCHITECTS>
FEUERSINGER ARCHITEKTUR // 2015.
HOUSE> 230 SQM // 10 + 2 GUESTS //
5 BEDROOMS // 4 BATHROOMS +
1 SHOWER IN THE SAUNA. ADDRESS>
SENNINGERFELD 8, BRAMBERG A.
WILDKOGEL, AUSTRIA.
WWW.AUFDALEITN8.AT

Auf da Leitn 8

BRAMBERG A. WILDKOGEL,
AUSTRIA

Auf da Leitn 8 is located in the heart of the High Tauern region right next to a skiing run in the midst of a vehicle-free hamlet 819 meters above sea level. The spirit of local chalets is reflected in a novel and understated way in the natural stone façade, larch wood shingles, and oak wood interior. The straight-lined design does not make the ambiance seem rustic but modern instead. Precise lines dominate the furniture and the only ornaments are found on the chairs that were made by hand based on traditional templates that grant the interior the right amount of a local touch. The wood shimmers in different hues depending on the light and livens up the rooms. The Corten steel cladding on the terraces is exposed to the seasons and develops a color range of its own. Up to twelve people can be comfortably accommodated in the 230-square-meter living space across three floors. In cool weather, the sauna with relaxation area on the first floor, the cozy living area with adjoining open kitchen and a large, solid oak table beckon. The crackle of wood in the fireplace right next door spreads cozy warmth. Floor-to-ceiling windows bring nature close – whether it's the snowstorm whistling around the house, the sunshine warming the stone façade, or the rain enveloping the house in lush greenery. Two terraces offer impressive views of the mountain panorama.

Kitchen area. Auf da Leitn 8 in winter.
The terrace. Living area with panoramic windows.

House view from garden. Terrace with panorama.
Bathroom. Floor plans. Exterior view with snow.

GETTING AROUND. WINTER ATTRACTIONS INCLUDE SKIING AND SLEDDING RIGHT OUTSIDE THE DOOR, SKI TOURS, ICE-SKATING, SNOW HIKING, CROSS-COUNTRY SKIING. NEARBY SKIING AREAS INCLUDE KITZBÜHEL PASS THURN (WORLD'S BEST SKI RESORT), ZILLERTALARENA, AND KITZSTEINHORN. SUMMER ATTRACTIONS INCLUDE HIKING, CLIMBING, MOUNTAIN BIKING, PARAGLIDING, SWIMMING, GOLFING, THE KRIMMLER WATERFALLS, AND THE CITIES OF SALZBURG, INNSBRUCK, AND MUNICH, WHICH CAN BE REACHED IN ABOUT 1.5 HOURS.

INFORMATION. ARCHITECT>
MARTIN GRUBER // 2019.
HOUSE> 65 SQM // 4 GUESTS //
1 BEDROOM // 1 BATHROOM.
ADDRESS> VERDINGS PARDELL 52,
KLAUSEN, ITALY.
HTTPS://FREIFORM.IT

*Floor-to-ceiling windows. View of the green roof
from the top.*

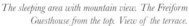

The sleeping area with mountain view. The Freiform Guesthouse from the top. View of the terrace.

Freiform Private Guesthouse

KLAUSEN, ITALY

In the heart of a stunning landscape in South Tyrol's Valle Isarco, nestled in the topography, lies a solitaire made of glass. Like a walk-in sculpture, the building nestles on its site and reveals the spatial structure, designed to fulfill the minimalist functions of a guesthouse, only when approached. The geometry stems from the creative intention to make a statement on the careful treatment of the landscape. Therefore, after the farm was handed over, it was converted into an organic farm and instead of the four potential vacation homes, a single, more private guesthouse was built.

It is only right before the entrance that the protected space reveals itself, that the glass body becomes visible under the green roof. A mobile external curtain protects the façade from view and sunlight. The ambivalence of the space is further enhanced by additionally planted fruit trees. Outdoor design gives the building stability and justifies the geometry of both floor and ceiling as a response to the immediate natural surroundings.

The interior consists of free-standing furniture; they zone the interflowing spaces. The 65-square-meter Freiform Guesthouse was furnished with high-quality materials such as oak and loden, whose warm feel perfectly balances the hard concrete and glass shell. The Freiform Guesthouse is masterfully executed by craftsmen companies of friends. It creates a particular charm by its sculptural design and is fully booked several months in advance.

Exterior view.
Exterior glass shell.

Interior view of the bathroom. The guesthouse nestled in the surrounding nature. Floor plan.

GETTING AROUND. WITHIN THIS SETTING, YOU HAVE THE OPPORTUNITY TO GO OFFLINE AND TO FOCUS ON NATURE AROUND YOU. A COVERED TERRACE AND TWO LOUNGERS UNDER OLD FRUIT TREES INVITE GUESTS TO DAYDREAM. IF YOU WANT TO BE PHYSICALLY ACTIVE HIKE TO THE LATZFONSER KREUZ OR TAKE A MTB TOUR ON ONE OF THE NUMEROUS ALPINE TRAILS. IN AUTUMN, TRADITIONAL TAVERNS INVITE GUESTS TO A TRADITIONAL "TÖRGGELEN" OFFERING NEW WINE, ROASTED CHESTNUTS AND CULINARY SPECIALTIES. IN WINTER, SKI TOURERS ENJOY A SUNNY ROUTE ON THE KÖNIGSANGER WITH A UNIQUE VIEW OF THE DOLOMITES.

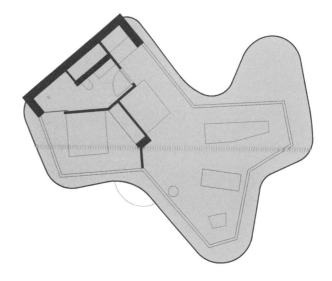

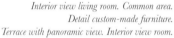
*Interior view living room. Common area.
Detail custom-made furniture.
Terrace with panoramic view. Interior view room.*

Miramonti Boutique Hotel

BOLZANO, ITALY

Only 20 minutes by car from the bustling city of Merano, the Miramonti Boutique Hotel resembles at first glance a rock jutting from the mountain. It is so cleverly integrated into nature with carefully chosen matching materials that this part of the hotel is almost entirely integrated into the dark mountain rock on which it is built. The dark outer skin immediately conveys intimacy and makes the clearly structured incisions of the terraces appear like ducts that lead into the depth. Inside the building, the extensive view resulting from the prominent position on the rock immediately catches the attention.

In the hall and the dining room only glass separates the guests from the horizon. On the extensive terrace too, nothing impedes the view and only an infinity pool at its outer edge stops

guests that do not suffer from vertigo. The generous terraces with floor-to-ceiling panoramic windows offer views of the surrounding green forests and mountain peaks. In 2017, the stargazing rooms were added, furnished in a satiated blue. Arranged under a multifaceted sloping roof, they expand the room experience in all dimensions.

INFORMATION. ARCHITECTS>
TARA ARCHITEKTEN – HEIKE POHL
AND ANDREAS ZANIER // 2021.
HOTEL> 5,200 SQM // 88 GUESTS //
44 BEDROOMS // 44 BATHROOMS.
ADDRESS> ST. KATHREINSTRASSE,
HAFLING, BOLZANO, ITALY.
WWW.HOTEL-MIRAMONTI.COM

GETTING AROUND. MERANO, THE CITY OF CULTURE WITH MANY HIDDEN VENUES, VARIOUS MARKETS AND RESTAURANTS HAS MUCH TO OFFER: THE THERMAL SPA, THE GARDENS OF TRAUTTMANSDORFF CASTLE, THE "ÖTZI" MUSEUM, THE LABYRINTH GARDEN, WINE TASTINGS AND HORSE RACES, ARE ALL EXPERIENCES NOT TO BE MISSED. VARIOUS LAKES INVITE SWIMMERS WITH THREE IMPRESSIVE WATERFALLS IN THE VICINITY. THE HIKING AREA MERAN 2000 OFFERS MANY TRAILS AND MOUNTAIN HUTS.

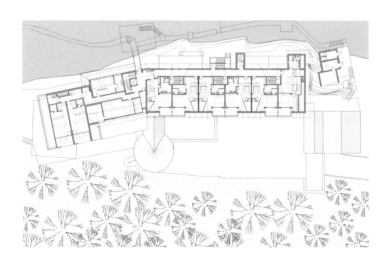

Panoramic view from the infinity pool.
Floor plan. View of the spa area.

Common living area.
Panoramic view from the wellness
area. Outdoor pool from above.

INFORMATION. ARCHITECTS>
ANAKO ARCHITECTURE // INTERIOR
DESIGN> SEBASTIAN HATZFELDT //
1688, RENOVATION 2013 AND 2021.
CHALET> 120 SQM // 4–6 GUESTS //
2 BEDROOMS // 2 BATHROOMS.
ADDRESS> GRANGENEUVE,
SAINT-MARTIN, VALAIS, SWITZERLAND.
WWW.CHALET-2-SPHÈRES.CH

Interior view of the living area. Chalet with
mountains. Main view from below. Exterior view.

Chalet-2-Sphères

VALAIS, SWITZERLAND

The name Chalet-2-Sphères derives from a second floor, dating from 1688, that was renovated in 2013, and from a firm modern basement. An old barn built in 1688 in block construction was dismantled one beam at a time. 20 kilometers from its previous location, a new basement was built first in exposed concrete, along with a new wood and steel substructure to support the old barn that was put on top of it. The historic beams were reassembled around the new substructure in their original way, including the old wooden posts with the overlying stones.

Through careful attention to detail and considerable effort, it was possible to save the historic barn and keep it as a witness of former times. The interior design carries and emphasizes those two different spheres of the old and the new.

In addition, the second floor offers an exquisite collection of up to 120-year-old stuffed animals (not hunting trophies), like those exhibited in natural history museums. There is a hidden home cinema with a 75" screen, a large audio system as well as an extensive library for good entertainment and cozy evenings.

Chalet from the garden. Bedroom with panoramic view. Living room. Panoramic window of the dining room. Floor plan.

GETTING AROUND. THE CHALET HAS AN EXTRAORDINARY UNUSUAL OPEN VIEW IN ALL DIRECTIONS AND UP TO THE GLACIERS AROUND THE DENT D'HÉRENS (4,171 M) IN THE SOUTH. AS FURTHER HIGHLIGHT, THERE ARE THREE ALPINE SETTLEMENTS SITUATED RIGHT ABOVE THE VALLEY, JUST LIKE IN A PICTURE BOOK. FROM OCTOBER TO THE BEGINNING OF NOVEMBER, THE LARCHES TURN GOLD. THIS IS AN INCREDIBLE INTENSE COLOR SPECTACLE. IN WINTER, THERE ARE BEAUTIFUL TRAILS AND A NUMBER OF DIFFERENT SKI RESORTS.

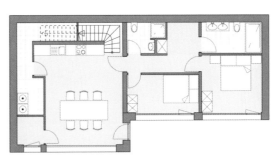

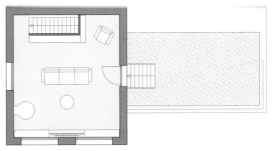

INFORMATION. ARCHITECTS>
OFIS ARCHITECTS // 2016.
CABIN> 9.7 SQM // 9 GUESTS.
ADDRESS> MOUNT KANIN,
SLOVENIA.
WWW.PZS.SI

Kanin Winter Cabin

MOUNT KANIN, SLOVENIA

Kanin Winter Cabin forms a compact wooden volume consisting of three platforms, which are suspended facing the valley. A panoramic window is the vertical limit, offering a breathtaking view of the surrounding mountain panorama. The geometry of the hut was designed to minimize the footprint on the rock, taking into account its weight and balance behavior. The interior is clad in wood and can accommodate up to nine mountaineers.

Design and construction of the hut required taking into account extreme weather conditions, drastic temperature changes, snow, landslides and rough terrain, which resulted in the very specific architectural design and structure. The location of the Kanin Winter Cabin can only be reached via climbing paths or by helicopter. This is why each module arrived by helicopter from the Slovenian Armed Forces and, due to bad weather conditions, could only be positioned and fixed in the third attempt. This project shows how a shelter that is necessary for people, can also be great architecture, a solitaire, a sculpture in harmony with the mountains, while respecting nature and being sustainable. The Kanin Winter Cabin is built with the help of donations and many hardworking volunteers.

Side view. Interior view of the cabin.
Front view. View from below.

Detail of the panoramic window. Side view.
Wooden interior. Model. Kanin Winter
Cabin from below.

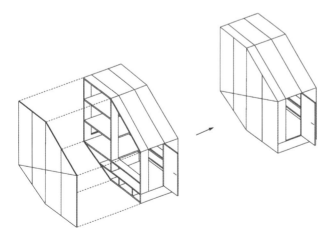

GETTING AROUND. KANIN IS A MOUNTAIN ABOVE THE SMALL TOWN OF BOVEC, WITH BEAUTIFUL RESORTS NEARBY. THE AREA IS ALSO RENOWNED FOR BATTLES THAT TOOK PLACE DURING WORLD WAR I WITH MANY REMAINS STILL FOUND IN THE AREA. THIS PARTICULAR SITE WAS CHOSEN BECAUSE OF ITS 360-DEGREE VIEWS OVER SLOVENIA AND ITALY, AND SPECTACULAR VIEWS TO TRIGLAV, SOCA VALLEY AND ADRIATIC SEA. IT IS A DESTINATION FOR HIKERS, CLIMBERS, CAVERS, MOUNTAINEERS, NATURE LOVERS AND ROMANTICS.

INFORMATION. ARCHITECTS>
NORBERT MARIA BRAUN / MUH2
GMBH AND JOHANNES HUMER –
ARCHITEKT – HANDGEDACHT ZT E.U.
// 2019. HUT> 40 AND 75 SQM // 2 AND
4–8 GUESTS // 1 BEDROOM AND 2
BEDROOMS + SLEEPING FLOOR //
1 AND 2 BATHROOMS.
ADDRESS> SCHÖNEBEN 23,
ULRICHSBERG, AUSTRIA.
WWW.RAMENAI.AT

Die Ramenai

The Ramenai is not a conventional holiday village of chalets. It is a place for those who seek relaxed simplicity and cherish an exciting fusion of forest and housing. Nine large and small chalets are located in a glade in the middle of the Bohemian Forest. The cottages, which were designed with great care for the essentials, reflect the traditions and life of the forest farmers and farmhands of the Mühlviertel region. It is their lifestyles that served as pattern for the concept of this unique forest village.

"With the Ramenai I want to show people that time and simplicity are the greatest luxury nowadays". It is precisely with this spirit that Günter Hofbauer, host at the Ramenai, has realized his vision of a simple and mindful lifestyle. The materials are genuine and cozy, the spaces are intentionally quite narrow, but just because of that very convincing. The cottages offer everything you need to spend an unforgettable time and "a bit" more. In the past there wasn't a sauna in each lodging. However, there used to be a traditional "Schwarzkuchl" fireplace, a modern version of which you can find in the new cottages. Out of respect for nature, a particularly environmentally friendly construction method was top priority. Therefore, neither concrete nor sealants were used at all. All craftmanship involved in the construction is from the Mühlviertel and its surroundings.

Exterior view. Interior view of the kitchen. Detail of the fireplace in the living area. Interior view.

A bedroom. Detail sauna. Living room.
Sketch of Waldlerdorf.

GETTING AROUND. A RESORT SURROUNDED BY A LOT OF UNTOUCHED NATURE. DISCOVERY TOURS, SUMMIT TOURS, PEDALING, CLIMBING, PADDLING OR SIMPLY WALKING THROUGH THE FOREST FOR THOSE WHO LIKE TO BE ACTIVE, THE BOHEMIAN FOREST OFFERS A WIDE RANGE OF ACTIVITIES. THE SKI AREA HIGHLFICHT IS ALSO ONLY 10 KM AWAY. RIGHT THERE, IN THE BORDER TRIANGLE BETWEEN AUSTRIA, BOHEMIA AND BAVARIA, YOU CAN EXPLORE A WONDERFUL, OLD CULTURAL LANDSCAPE AND REDISCOVER SOME ALMOST FORGOTTEN THINGS. OLD HANDICRAFTS, ANCESTRAL KNOWLEDGE AND ROMANTIC PLACES ARE EXTRAORDINARY AND WORTH A VISIT.

Ramenai from the forest.
Interior view of the dining area.

INFORMATION. ARCHITECT>
MICHELE DE LUCCHI // 2020.
HOTEL> 700 SQM // 12 GUESTS //
6 BEDROOMS // 6 BATHROOMS +
1 SAUNA. ADDRESS> OBERRADEIN 59,
REDAGNO, ITALY.
WWW.ZIRMERHOF.COM

Interior view living room.
View of the kitchen. Private balcony.
Exterior view Häuser der Wiese.

The complex with mountains.
Interior view.

Häuser der Wiese Zirmerhof

REDAGNO, ITALY

The historic rooms of the Zirmerhof are complemented by new, exclusive living rooms. A linear maisonette and a small circular pavilion on the meadow in front of the historic courtyard are placed in such a way that they do not interfere with the view from the terrace and the other rooms of the existing building.

Being a modern interpretation of the traditional hay barns, they perfectly fit into their context; large openings provide a view to the wonderful nature. Both houses have a round roof, without edges or peaks, and are covered with a light coating of larch shingles. The rooms are located on the first floor with direct access to the meadow as well as on the second floor, which according to the historical model, is located directly in front of the paved forecourt. The attic is the first floor, as it used to be in the times of the old stables: the cows lived downstairs while the hay was stored upstairs. In both buildings a single material dominates: the structure, the roof shingles, the interior walls, the doors, the windows, and the furniture are all made of wood. This not only represents a sustainable and traditional construction, but also generates a lot of warmth and comfort. The design, which is based on the location itself, picks up on the old philosophy of the Zirmerhof: every detail deserves attention and is developed with care. "Wherever you look, the mind finds peace."

Exterior view entrance. Detail of the bathroom.
Interior view of a room.

Room with panoramic window. Detail of the gallery.
Exterior view of the ensemble.

GETTING AROUND. THE SURROUNDINGS OFFER A LOT OF PLACES TO GO: THE BLETTERBACH GORGE TOGETHER WITH THE ENTIRE GEOPARC, IS CONSIDERED A UNIQUE PLACE ALL OVER EUROPE. THERE ARE ALSO CASTLES AND FORTRESSES, A SCULPTURE TRAIL, THE DÜRER TRAIL AND MUSEUMS. ALL ALONG THE WINE ROUTE, ESTATES AND WINERIES WELCOME GUESTS FOR A VISIT AND WINE TASTING. YOU CAN TAKE DAY TRIPS TO LAKE GARDA, THE LAGOON CITY OF VENICE, MANTUA OR VERONA TO EXPERIENCE THE CULTURE AND LIFESTYLE OF NORTHERN ITALY.

Map of the Alps

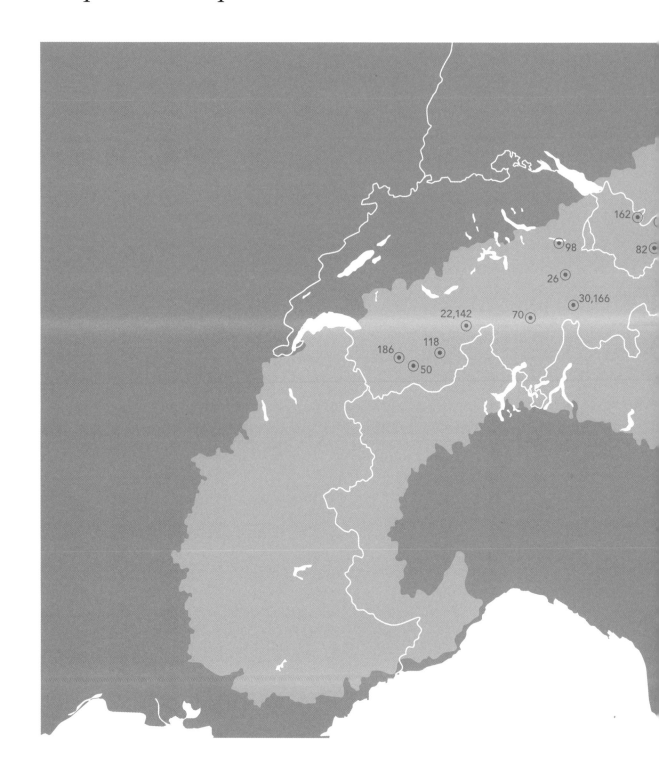

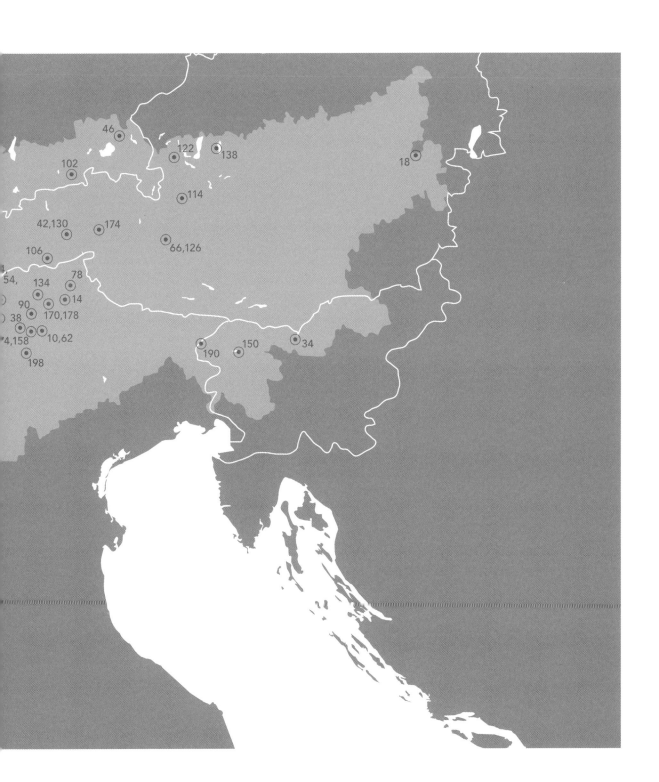

Picture
Credits

All other pictures were made available
by the architects, designers, or hosts.

Cover front: Tobias Kaser Photography,
Brixen. Cover back (from left to right,
from above to below): Andre Schönherr,
Alan Bianchi, Alex Filz, Gustav Willeit.

The Deutsche Nationalbibliothek lists this
publication in the Deutsche Nationalbib-
liografie; detailed bibliographic data are
available on the Internet at http://dnb.dnb.de

ISBN 978-3-03768-270-8
© 2022 by Braun Publishing AG
www.braun-publishing.ch

1st edition 2022

Editor: Sibylle Kramer
Editorial staff and layout:
María Barrera del Amo, Alessia Calabrò
Translation: Sandra Ellegiers
Graphic concept: Michaela Prinz, Berlin
Reproduction: Bild1Druck GmbH, Berlin